CW00549117

The Royal Law
Source of our Freedom Today

The Royal Law

Source of our Freedom Today

L L Blake

SHEPHEARD-WALWYN

First published in 2000 by
Shepheard-Walwyn (Publishers) Ltd
Suite 604, The Chandlery
50 Westminster Bridge Road
London SE1 7QY

British Library Cataloguing in Publication Data
A catalogue record of this book
is available from the British Library

ISBN 0 85683 191 3

Typeset by R E Clayton
Printed in Great Britain by Redwood Books,
Trowbridge

Contents

Dedicated to all those who believe in the traditions of our society

Acknowledgements

The author and publisher gratefully acknowledge the
permission given by HM Stationery Office to quote
extensively from *The Form and Order of the Coronation
Service* for Her Majesty Queen Elizabeth II, 2 June 1953.
They also acknowledge the kind permission of
Chetham's Library, Manchester, to reproduce the
thirteenth century illustration of the
Coronation of King John on the jacket.

Here is Wisdom; This is the royal Law; These are the lively Oracles of God.

The presenting of the Holy Bible, Coronation Service

More than 70% of Britons affirm belief in God, but not as churchgoers

Religion in Britain since 1945, Grace Davie
(Oxford 1994)

Our whole history and culture in Europe is based on Christianity, whether you believe in it or not. Our culture is Christian: Shakespeare, Mozart, – all that makes life worth living is part of the Christian tradition.

Sir John Mortimer, *playwright and atheist.*
(*Daily Telegraph* 28.4.99)

1

Government

This book is to do with words of government. Disraeli once said: 'With words we govern men'.[1] An Act of Parliament is an act in words. Even brute force requires a commander's voice. Solzhenitsyn put it accurately enough, when he foretold the break-up of the Soviet regime:[2]

> Yes, yes, of course – we all know that you cannot poke a stick through the walls of a concrete tower, but here's something to think about: what if those walls are only a painted backdrop?

> Looking back, even a fool would be able to predict it today: the Soviet regime could certainly have been breached only by literature. The regime has been reinforced with concrete to such an extent that neither a military coup nor a political organisation nor a picket line of strikers can knock it over or run it through. Only the solitary writer would be able to do this...

In the appendix to this book is printed a substantial part of the Coronation Service for Her Majesty Queen Elizabeth II. Reader, you are asked to read it, before proceeding any further; and to drink deeply of the magnificent words. At one point in the Service, the Archbishop goes to the Queen's chair and says: 'Our gracious Queen: to keep your Majesty ever mindful of the Law and the Gospel of God as the Rule for the whole life and government of Christian princes, we present you with this Book, the most valuable thing that this world affords'. And the Moderator of the General Assembly of the Church of Scotland presents the Bible to the Queen, and says: 'Here is Wisdom; This is the royal Law;

---

1. *Churchill* edited by Robert Blake and Wm. Roger Louis, [OUP 1993], p .6
2. *The Oak and the Calf,* [Collins and Harvill Press 1980], p. 10

These are the lively oracles of God'.

Are these meaningless words in the modern world? Do they have a strange beauty about them, as coming from a distant past of coronation-making, but no relevance to our lives today? Are we governed by them any more? Is there a Government of God?

In the view of this writer, there is.

Take an ordinary example: here is part of Regulation 83 of the Motor Vehicles (Construction and Use) Regulations, 1969[1]:

> (1) Save as provided in paragraph (2) of this Regulation, no person shall use or cause or permit to be used on a road, any motor vehicle or trailer a wheel of which is fitted with a pneumatic tyre, if...

> (f) where the tyre is fitted to a wheel of a motor vehicle, being a motor cycle whereof the cylinder capacity of the engine does not exceed 50 cubic centimetres, the tread of the tyre does not show throughout at least three quarters of the breadth of the tread and round the entire outer circumference of the tyre a pattern the relief of which is clearly visible, or where the tyre is fitted to the wheel of any other motor vehicle or any trailer, the tread pattern (excluding any tie-bar) of the tyre does not have a depth of at least 1mm. throughout at least three-quarters of the breadth of the tread and round the entire outer circumference of the tyre;

A dense enough Regulation to measure out the responsibility of those who do not obey their duty to others. Yet, at any time, we can be free of this density by simply observing the rule of the Common Law:[2]

> The duty of the owner of a motor car in a highway...is to use reasonable care to avoid injuring those using the highway.

And lying beyond that:[3]

> Master, which is the great commandment in the law?
> Jesus said unto him, Thou shalt love the Lord thy God with all thy heart,

---

1. S.I. 1969 No 321, as amended.
2. as expressed e.g. by Atkin LJ in *Hambrook v Stokes Bros.* [1925] 1KB 141
3. *St Matthew* 22, vv 36-40

and with all thy soul, and with all thy mind.
This is the first and great commandment.
And the second is like unto it, Thou shalt love thy neighbour as thyself.
On these two commandments hang all the law and the prophets.

Jean Domat, the seventeenth century French lawyer, wrote something of great value concerning these two laws, love thy God, love thy neighbour:[1]

> However, although men have violated these fundamental laws, and although society be in a state strangely different from that which ought to be raised upon these foundations, and cemented by this union; it is still true that these divine laws, which are essential to the nature of Man, remain immutable, and have never ceased to oblige men to the observance of them; and it is likewise certain... that all the laws which govern society, even in the condition in which it is at present, are no other than consequences of these first laws.

'All the laws': he makes no exception. It is a true lawyer's perspective, looking down the line from the very finest to the coarsest. Yet the fundamental rules remain, and are still there, in the twenty-first as in the seventeenth century. They can always be appealed to, when we lose our way, and sincerely want to turn back.

In 1917, in *Bowman v Secular Society*[2], the House of Lords in its wisdom decided that Christianity was no longer part of the law of England. Quite how they made this out it is hard to say; but it was the heyday of Fabianism. Lord Sumner gave the leading judgment: 'My Lords, with all respect for the great names of the lawyers who had used it, the phrase "Christianity is part of the law of England" is really not law: it is rhetoric...One asks what part of our law may Christianity be, and what part of Christianity may it be that is part of our law? Chief Justice Best once said that "there is no act which Christianity forbids that the law will not reach. If it were otherwise, Christianity would not be, as it has always been

---

1. *The Civil Law in its Natural Order*, Vol. 1, Chap. 1, sect. viii
2. [1917] AC 406

held to be, part of the law of England". But this was rhetoric too'.

Rhetoric or not, they had their minds changed for them by that excellent Welsh judge, Lord Atkin, in 1932, in the most famous case in English law (although its facts took place in Scotland), *Donoghue v Stevenson*[1]. There Mrs Donoghue claimed that she had been poisoned by a decomposed snail which had floated out of an opaque ginger beer bottle, when she poured herself a second drink, in a cafe in Paisley. The matter went as high as the House of Lords for a final decision as to whether there was a cause of action, on these alleged facts (although subsequently there was never a trial on the evidence). Judges simply did not know what to do: there was a great sympathy for the woman's plight, but the state of the existing law did not seem to provide any remedy. She could not sue the cafe: the drink had been purchased by someone else and, in any event, how could the snail have been detected in an opaque bottle? Should the manufacturer be liable? But there appeared to be no nexus between him and the victim; the bottle was not, by nature, a dangerous commodity for which he could be held liable *per se*.

In the biography *Lord Atkin*[2] it is mentioned that Atkin did not think that a more important problem had ever occupied the House of Lords in its judicial capacity. The appeal raised a question which had revolutionary consequences for the law of civil liability for carelessness. 'It provided a test for the legal system and would demonstrate whether that system was congruent with or remote from the everyday needs of society'.

Atkin himself was searching for some general principle which would open the law. His eldest grandson, now Lord Aldington, remembers as a boy how he attended the family lunch party in Wales:

1. [1932] AC 562
2. by Geoffrey Lewis [Butterworths 1983] p. 57 *et seq.*

During the summer holidays of 1931 I was staying at Craig-y-don with other members of the family. In those days the family went to Matins at the Aberdovey Church every Sunday morning and there was a large family lunch with aunts and cousins presided over by my grandfather, who took much pride in his carving of the joint. He often used the carving time and the carving weapons to conduct a discussion. I remember on several occasions that the post-church discussion about the snail and the ginger beer bottle case– who is my neighbour? – was an easily understandable theme immediately after church. I was then at Winchester aged 17 – an enthusiastic classical student and ignorant of the law, but fascinated by the arguments, and proud of having a grandfather who was so concerned with human relationships and responsibilities...

In Lord Atkin's speech giving judgment in the House of Lords, the great principle emerges: '...The rule that you are to love your neighbour becomes in law, you must not injure your neighbour; and the lawyer's question, Who is my neighbour? receives a restricted reply. You must take reasonable care to avoid acts or omissions which you can reasonably foresee would be likely to injure your neighbour. Who, then, in law is my neighbour? The answer seems to be – persons who are so closely and directly affected by my act that I ought reasonably to have them in contemplation as being so affected when I am directing my mind to the acts or omissions which are called in question.'

Later, Lord Atkin was to say: 'I doubt whether the whole of the law of tort could not be comprised in the golden maxim to do unto your neighbour as you would that he should do unto you'.

Thus, the opinions of the most senior judges in the realm meant that there was a cause of action for Mrs Donoghue to take up. She was the neighbour whom the manufacturer had reasonably to keep in mind when he was making and bottling his product. The Common Law thereafter was opened to all manner of actions in negligence, where the care bestowed on one's neighbour falls short of the standard of reasonableness required by the law. Indeed, the law was revolutionized. But it had as its foundation the revealed law, the law from the scriptures of God. 'It will be an advantage', said Lord Atkin at the end of his judgment, 'to make it clear that the law in this matter as in most others is in accordance with sound common sense'.

The Will of God is law for us, and our true government, and it finds expression through words. As St John said:[1]

> In the beginning was the Word, and the Word was with God, and the Word was God.
> The same was in the beginning with God.
> All things were made by him; and without him was not any thing made that was made.
> In him was life; and the life was the light of men.
> And the light shineth in darkness; and the darkness comprehended it not...
> And the Word was made flesh, and dwelt among us (and we beheld his glory, the glory as of the only begotten of the Father), full of grace and truth.

Jean Domat made the point that the divine laws are essential to the nature of Man, and are immutable. What, then, is the true nature of Man? The eighteenth century explored this subject very thoroughly. They came to the conclusion that Man's true nature was to be happy; and this happiness (or inner peace and harmony) was prescribed by the Creator through natural laws, discoverable by the use of reason.

One of the best descriptions comes from the seminal work of our great Common Law jurist, Sir William Blackstone (1723-80). In his *Commentaries on the Laws of England* Blackstone writes:[2]

> For [the Creator] has so intimately connected, so inseparably woven the laws of eternal justice with the happiness of each individual, that the latter cannot be attained but by observing the former; and if the former be punctually obeyed, it cannot but induce the latter. In consequence of

---

1. *St John* 1, vv 1-5, 14
2. Vol. 1, Introduction, sect. 2

which mutual connection of justice and human frailty, he has not perplexed the law of nature with a multitude of abstracted rules and precepts...but has graciously reduced the rule of obedience to this one paternal precept, "that man should pursue his own true and substantial happiness". This is the foundation of what we call ethics, or natural law. For the several articles into which it is branched in our systems, amount to no more than demonstrating that this or that action tends to man's real happiness, and therefore very justly concluding that the performance of it is a part of the law of nature; or, on the other hand, that this or that action is destructive of man's real happiness, and therefore that the law of nature forbids it.

Jeremy Bentham, who was one of Blackstone's students, was incensed by what he considered to be the Tory complacency of his tutor. No doubt others, reading this today, would be equally cross. Happiness, Bentham snorted, went without question: everyone desired happiness, few would find it. He desired 'to show how absolutely unserviceable and indeed disserviceable the idea of God is for the purpose of solving any political problem, and to point out the absurdity of jumbling in the manner [Blackstone] has done, things sacred with profane'.[1]

In due course Bentham adopted and propounded the principle behind Utilitarianism (which still motivates us today), that 'the greatest happiness of the greatest number is the foundation of morals and legislation'. Blackstone said, quite rightly, that the test was in the *effect* or *result* of one's actions: did it produce happiness, or harmony? On this test, ever since the eighteenth century, Bentham's pronouncement has been gravely deficient in two respects: welfare state legislation has divided people – while the 'greatest number' might be materially better off, and 'happy', the minority will be in misery; and it is certainly true that determining the nature and extent of that 'greatest happiness' has become the role and function of numerous political busybodies. Bentham himself, of course, was always designing ways of imposing his

---

1. *A Comment on the Commentaries* Sect. 3, 'Divine Law'.

ideas of happiness on the multitude.

Blackstone's test was, and is, an exact one. The question is whether any law, written or unwritten, statute or custom, makes everyone happy. That is to say, they all agree with, and live harmoniously with, the operation of that law. As Plato said, ... 'the object of laws... is to make those who use them happy, for all goods are derived from them'.[1] On the other hand, if a law divides the community, makes some happy and others miserable, this is by definition not a law natural to Man. Being unnatural, it can be law only for a limited time, and will have constantly to be amended and changed, to utter complexity and confusion. Then there is a chance to revert to the underlying natural law, which never uses force to achieve its ends, but just works all the time. It is the law we all take for granted, like gravity. But it is immutable and it runs our lives, basically.

This view - that natural law in fact runs our lives for us - may not be a popular one. Yet, to Socrates, it was self-evident. Condemned unjustly to die, he is visited in his cell by friends who urge him to escape. He replies, but why should I shun the laws which at the beginning gave me life, and protected and maintained me, when now they have decided I must die? He pretends that the laws of Athens speak to him:[2]

> 'Consider, Socrates, if we are speaking truly that in your present attempt you are going to do us an injury. For, after having brought you into the world, and nurtured and educated you, and given you and every other citizen a share in every good which we had to give, we further proclaim to every Athenian, that if he does not like us when he has come of age and has seen the ways of the city, and made our acquaintance, he may go where he pleases and take his goods with him; and none of us laws will interfere with him... But he who has experience of the manner in which we order justice and administer the state, and still remains, has

1. *The Laws,* 631 [Jowett Translation].
2. *Crito,* 51-2 [Jowett Translation].

entered into an implied contract that he will do as we command him. And he who disobeys us is, we maintain, thrice wrong; first, because in disobeying us he is disobeying his parents; secondly, because we are the authors of his education; thirdly, because he has made an agreement with us that he will duly obey our commands; and he neither obeys them nor convinces us that our commands are unjust; and we do not rudely impose them, but give him the alternative of obeying or convincing us; - that is what we offer, and he does neither'.

Modern examples of those laws which divide people include abortion and divorce statutes. But underlying all activity in this country, and the English-speaking world generally, is the Common Law of reason, the natural law which we tend to take for granted. How often do we buy travel tickets on buses and trains without considering the law of contract? For that matter our daily purchases and sales are all governed by the law of sale of goods, which we only hear about when something goes wrong; and then there is the possibility of a court hearing in which the wrong may be righted, by a judgment based on reason (or appealed). We pass and re-pass along the public highway without considering the thicket of laws through which we go. We travel by car and public transport, knowing that the law of torts protects us from careless injury. No one can enter our house without permission or the authority of a court. We do not leave our homes in the morning, only to find them occupied by another family on our return. We take the law of property for granted; but there are countries where history has shown the evils of dispossession of rightful owners, to be replaced by favoured ethnic groupings.

There is a third factor in this triad of evidence of the existence of God's government, starting with the divine commandment, going on through natural law – and that is, rightness. We know in ourselves what is right and what is wrong. It is implanted. J E G de Montmorency, sometime Quain Professor of Comparative Law in the University of London, said this in his book:

But if a man or woman, however bad, were placed in a position that eliminated all personal interest and were asked to decide whether such an action were right or wrong the *mens conscia recti* that dwells in every one of us would prevail, at any rate prevail to the extent that the answer would be that this action would be right and that action would be wrong, though they themselves would defy the consequences of a wrong action...It is a strange and mysterious thing, this universal sense of what is right, a sense that cannot be obscured in any ultimate resort in any human being... It is a mysterious thing, but the explanation is really not far to seek in an age that recognizes that law - universality of operation - is the very atmosphere of all our being.

...It would be a more mysterious and stranger thing if there were not the universal sense of orderliness, and for this reason: it would be an exception from an otherwise all-prevailing rule in the universe as we know it. The material universe, the conventional structure of which is slowly becoming known to us, is incapable of deviation from a certain orderliness which can scarcely be an accidental thing, which certainly is an inherent property of physical energy, which certainly is reasonable in our human sense, an orderliness which many or most people attribute to a self-conscious external Mind closely concerned with the affairs of the universe, a Mind which we call God.[1]

Around the walls of the fifteenth century Platonic Academy in Florence was inscribed the maxim of the philosopher-priest, Marsilio Ficino: 'All things are directed from goodness to goodness. Rejoice in the present; set no value on property, seek no honours. Avoid excess; avoid activity. Rejoice in the present.'[2]

It is this rightness which is equity in the law and sovereignty in government. Equity, originating in the Sanskrit 'eka', meaning 'one', is that which gives wholeness, justice, to the law when its balance is found wanting. Similarly, sovereignty in government means doing right to the people, or, better still, letting right be done; for right is always in the intention of God, as we can see in the above quotation from Ficino. What is required from govern-

---

1. *The Principles of Law* [Benn's Sixpenny Library 1929] pp. 11-13
2. *The Letters of Marsilio Ficino* [Shepheard-Walwyn] Vol. 1, p. 40

ment is simply to remove those obstacles which stand in the way of goodness flowing to goodness. The historic Petition of Right was a means by which the subject might bring the Crown under law, culminating in the endorsement by the Home Secretary of the words 'Let right be done'.

'Upon that difference', wrote Professor R W Chambers, '- whether or no we place Divine Law in the last resort above the law of the State - depends the whole future of the world'.[1]

Marsilio Ficino (1433-99), upon whose teaching in a very real sense the whole direction and purpose of the present Renaissance culture depended, makes the same point:[2]

> ...For I have learned from Plato that those arts which are concerned with personal welfare may sometimes be adequately directed by human wisdom; but that in the art which looks after the good of the state, the director is God Himself and should be acknowledged as such. I have learned that to God belongs the care of all things, but especially of public and state affairs, and that human wisdom is not the governess, but rather the handmaid and servant of divine government.
>
> The Platonic myth in *Protagoras* alludes to this: Prometheus, or human providence, discovered all the arts except care of the state. For this, he says, is given to us by Jupiter through Mercury; that is, it is granted by divine providence through angelic inspiration day by day. Plato also alludes to this by means of comparison: just as without man one beast cannot be successfully and rightly guided by another, so without God man cannot be guided by man. What else could this prophecy mean: 'The king's heart is in the hand of the Lord and He turneth it whithersoever He will'? Likewise this saying from the gospels: 'Thou couldst have no power except it were given thee from above'; and again: 'There is no power but of God: the powers that be are ordained of God'. Dionysius the Areopagite made archangels teachers and guides to the leaders of men. David used the Psalms as reins to regulate the government of his kingdom. For he knew that 'except the Lord keep the city, the watch-

---

1. *Under God and the Law* [Basil Blackwell 1949], cover note.
2. *The Letters of Marsilio Ficino op. cit.*, Vol. V, pp 50-51

man waketh but in vain'. Solomon represents divine wisdom as pro-
claiming: 'By me kings reign and lawgivers decree what is just. By me
princes rule and the mighty decree justice'…
Orators and poets wisely say that those who hold public office are like
the helmsmen of ships and, like those who are forever tossed among
rocks by wind and wave, they are perpetually in need of protection by
divine powers…

As 'David used the Psalms to regulate the government of his
kingdom', so we use the Coronation Service as reins to regulate
the true government of this kingdom. At the heart of the constitution of this country is, therefore, a song of praise.

It is all a matter of words. Fine words give rise to fine actions;
the proliferation of hollowed-out words gives rise to confusion and
doubt. Indeed, words can be so manipulated by government that
they express the opposite of what they were created to do: the best
examples come from George Orwell's frighteningly perceptive
book, *1984*. Winston is looking out of his window at the white
walls of the Ministry of Truth, on which are emblazoned the words:

WAR IS PEACE

FREEDOM IS SLAVERY

IGNORANCE IS STRENGTH[1]

Meanings are not only distorted, but the language is compacted
into Newspeak so that concepts of liberty are forgotten. Winston's
acquaintance, Syme, works on the eleventh edition of the Newspeak Dictionary. In the foul canteen of the Ministry of Truth,
Syme speaks enthusiastically of his work:[2]

'Don't you see that the whole aim of Newspeak is to narrow the range
of thought? In the end we shall make thoughtcrime literally impossible,
because there will be no words in which to express it. Every concept that
can ever be needed will be expressed by exactly *one* word, with its

1. [Penguin Books], p. 29
2. *Ibid.*, p. 55

meaning rigidly defined and all its subsidiary meanings rubbed out and forgotten. Already, in the Eleventh Edition, we're not far from that point. But the process will still be continuing long after you and I are dead. Every year fewer and fewer words, and the range of conscious-ness always a little smaller...'

That must be the great fear, that the 'range of consciousness' becomes ever smaller, and 'political correctness' rules the mind. The way forward must be through literature, as Solzhenitsyn reminds us. Children should be encouraged to read the best litera-ture, especially Shakespeare, the King James Bible and - the Cor-onation Service. P D James wrote: 'Give people language and you give them control over their lives'.[1]

The language of the Prayer Book and of the Coronation Serv-ice is the language of true government, which goes on all the time behind the facade of party politics. It is the language at the heart of the great, historic institutions, many of which are the product of medieval thinking, now so derided; but which have survived Ref-ormation and Renaissance and are the foundation on which the modern state cavorts – these institutions are monarchy, parlia-ment, common law, jury system, church, universities, civil service, armed forces. Monarchy is consecrated to its lifelong duty through the words of the Coronation Service, and, in particular, the oath; the common law at its finest is expressed in words of poetic beauty. Indeed, Blackstone's work, *The Commentaries*, was once described as the poetry of law. The Church has Tyndale. Universities - the old universities - are centres for the teaching of universal knowledge,[2] not for instruction in how to make money. The civil service traditionally sought its recruits among those with classical learning. The Navy went into battle with flags signalling fine words, 'England expects that every man will do his duty'.

We need from time to be reminded of the existence of these

---

1. *The Salisbury Review*, Summer 1999, p. 5
2. *The Idea of a University*, John Henry Newman [Oxford], preface.

institutions and to know that they form the essence of the nation. A *Times* leader, headed 'National Interest', once said:[1]

> The sovereign state of Britain is the Crown in Parliament. The system of parliamentary democracy embraces the notion of governments formed from parliamentary majorities for limited periods of office, with regular provision for peaceful change when the parliamentary majority reflects a different balance of political interest. To be loyal to the principles of parliamentary democracy involves a residual disloyalty to the government of the day since it must imply acceptance that a different government with different policies from the present one would also command the same loyalty from its servants and from the other state institutions as this one does…ministers may have their Parliamentary majority behind them and it may give them temporary power to use the permanent institutions of the state - the monarchy, the civil service, the armed forces - to further their policies. But those institutions will outlast them and be at the service of their political opponents.

Even as the words of the Coronation Service may nourish us, so they nourish these institutions which give life to the nation.

Compare the language with which this country entered the Second World War with that bellowed from Berlin. King George VI told the nation: 'We can only do the right as we see the right, and reverently commit our cause to God'. Hitler to his Army of the West and to the German people: 'Sections of the German Army in the East have now, for two days, in response to Polish attacks, been fighting for the establishment of a peace which shall assure life and freedom to the German people. If you do your duty, the battle in the East will have reached its successful conclusion in a few months, and then the power of the whole Nazi State stands behind you'.[2]

Lord Denning, that great master of the law, was also a master of language. At the end of one of his books he said:

---

1. 25th February 1985
2. quoted in *Sovereignty – Power beyond Politics*, L L Blake [Shepheard-Walwyn 1988], p. 89

[I]f we seek truth and justice we cannot find it by argument and debate, nor by reading and thinking, but only by the maintenance of true religion and virtue. Religion concerns the spirit in man whereby he is able to recognize what is truth and what is justice; whereas law is only the application, however imperfectly, of truth and justice in our everyday affairs. If religion perishes in the land, truth and justice will also. We have already strayed too far from the faith of our fathers. Let us return to it, for it is the only thing that can save us.[1]

Just as American children learn about their Constitution, so we should remind ourselves (and particularly our children) of the fine quality of the Coronation Service; and it is the purpose of this book so to remind us. Edward Ratcliff, in his account of *The English Coronation Service*,[2] wrote:

In a sense, the English Coronation Service epitomizes the history of the English monarchy and people, and of the relation existing between them. What we collect piecemeal from historical and constitutional documents, scattered over a period of nearly a thousand years, we find gathered up and integrated in the Coronation Service.

The Coronation Service is where the Divine Law is placed above the law of the State, acknowledged and reverenced. It reminds us of the source of all our law, in truth and in justice. We should not forget the words in which are conveyed the truth which inspires our Common Law.

The question is, whether this fine language can continue into the next coronation, when it comes – given the sorry propensity of the Church to desecrate its own liturgy. Fortunately, the oath by a new monarch committed to a lifetime's obedience is embedded in an Act of Parliament (the Coronation Oath Act 1689).

HRH Prince Charles loves the English language and is unlikely to make any major changes to the Service.

---

1. *The Changing Law* [Stevens 1953], p. 122
2. SPCK 1937, pp 20-1

2

Monarchy

The 'Government of God' must ultimately prevail in human affairs. Indeed, most people seem to have an idea it exists – the quotation at the beginning of this book asserts that 'more than 70% of Britons affirm belief in God, but not as church-goers'. In all probability the statistic in the United States of America would show the majority *are* churchgoers. It follows, if they think about it, that God must have a hand in governing them, at least in the making of their moral choices. Lord Denning once said:[1] 'Without religion there can be no morality; and without morality there can be no law'. That is to say, if I understand him correctly, unless there is understanding of the difference between right and wrong, no amount of man-made law will do any good. Yet right and wrong are established by the scriptures.

The day to day political government may use the powers of the historic institutions - monarchy, parliament, common law, etc. - wisely or foolishly. It may - and very often does - interfere with the natural, God-given operation of these powers, frequently without any idea of their origin or purpose. For instance, the political government may seek to destroy the House of Lords, which is the meeting place of those historic institutions. It will run up against difficulties: mainly because there is a natural balance of forces, eloquently described by Blackstone:[2]

> A body of nobility is also more peculiarly necessary in our mixed and compounded constitution, in order to support the rights of both the crown and the people, by forming a barrier to withstand the encroachments of

---

1. *The Changing Law* [Stevens 1953], p.99
2. *The Commentaries*, Book I, chap. 2

both. It creates and preserves that gradual scale of dignity, which proceeds from the peasant to the prince; rising like a pyramid from a broad foundation, and diminishing to a point as it rises. It is this ascending and contracting proportion that adds stability to any government; for when the departure is sudden from one extreme to another, we may pronounce that state to be precarious. The nobility are therefore the pillars, which are reared from among the people, more immediately to support the throne; and if that falls, they must also be buried under its ruins. Accordingly, when in the last century the commons had determined to extirpate monarchy, they also voted the House of Lords to be useless and dangerous...

According to Tanner[1] at the time of the restoration of the monarchy, 'On April 25 [1660] the two Houses met again after the old order, the Peers once more returning to Westminster. On May 1 they took into consideration the Declaration from Breda... a vote was carried that "according to the ancient and fundamental laws of this kingdom, the government is and ought to be by King, Lords, and Commons"'. You interfere with those 'ancient and fundamental laws' at your peril. As Edmund Burke once said, 'To innovate is not to reform'.[2]

Tanner goes on to describe the entry into London of the restored monarch:

"With a triumph of above 20,000 horse and foot, brandishing their swords and shouting with inexpressible joy; the ways strewed with flowers, the bells ringing, the streets hung with tapestry, fountains running with wine... I stood in the Strand and beheld it", continues Evelyn, "and blessed God. And all this was done without one drop of blood shed, and by that very army which rebelled against him; but it was the Lord's doing...

"Were you here", wrote another Londoner to a friend in Paris, "you would say, good God! Do the same people inhabit England that were in it ten or twenty years ago? Believe me, I know not whether I am in England or no, or whether I dream".

---

1. *English Constitutional Conflicts of the 17th Century* [Cambridge 1928] pp 208-9
2. *A Letter to a Noble Lord* [1796]

The above seems to indicate that one should be very careful of attempting to change the historic institutions of the English. Even after these institutions are abandoned, by edict of the rulers, they have a habit of emerging again, in much the same form as when they disappeared.

Political governments, anyway, are not particularly effective: Harold Lever describes their frustration:[1]

> The Cabinets of the period 1964-70 contained an unusually large proportion of highly gifted individuals. Why then was so little achieved? [The ex-minister Barbara] Castle...thinks that the failure was due to the defects of individual Ministers, notably Callaghan and Wilson. In my view she is wrong. These governments, like most other modern governments, overestimated their ability to shape and manage the complex drives of a mature economy. They wrongly assumed that they understood all the reasons for its shortcomings and so, not surprisingly, were all too ready to lay hands on superficial remedies for overcoming them. And all this without any attempt to understand the economics of an increasingly interdependent world. It is significant that the National Plans, which were no more than a summary of Labour Party rhetoric, ultimately enjoyed the derision even of the Cabinet itself. The real world and its occupants obstinately refused to conform to the encapsulations of reality on which election manifestos are based. This failure to recognise the limits of government action perhaps explains why the more vigorous the actions by governments to reverse Britain's economic decline, the more likely it is that the decline will be accelerated. I suppose it is too much to hope that politicians should not intoxicate themselves with the ambitious and perfectionist rhetoric of Opposition which implies that every problem has a neat and effective solution if only they were in office to put it into operation. I suppose it is idle to hope that any government will enter office with open humility seeking the modest prizes offered by reality rather than noble but purely notional goals. Such a government would find itself with successes denied to the self-righteous or the opinionated.

Such a revelation, by an experienced and highly intelligent pol-

---

1. *The Listener*, 22/11/84, pp 24-25

itician, is unsurprising, given that the socialist governments of those years were approaching the end of a cycle of collectivism. In about 1975, a swing of the pendulum brought in a new era, this time of individualism. Politicians as such cannot do much about the swings of public opinion. These swings are fashioned more by 'the ideas of economists and philosophers, both when they are right and when they are wrong... Practical men, who believe themselves to be quite exempt from any intellectual influences, are usually the slaves of some defunct economist'.[1] So, for a generation after the Second World War, political direction was given by the work of Keynes and Beveridge, and their collectivist ideas ruled, whatever the political complexion of the party in power. But in 1945 the young Margaret Roberts and Keith Joseph were reading a book which had just been published, *The Road to Serfdom*, by an Austrian economist, F A Hayek. His free market ideas were to be realised some 30 years later, in the premiership of Margaret Thatcher, as she became. Alexandre Kojève, who died in 1968, might be the prophet of our next age, of 'anonymous supranational administration', according to John Laughland in *The Times* (21/9/99).

This seems, historically, to be the way the pendulum swings, between individualism and collectivism. It is, in a way, purely mechanical.

In his book, *Law and Public Opinion in England*,[2] our great constitutional scholar, A V Dicey, described the process thus:

> Legislative opinion must be the opinion of the day, because, when laws are altered, the alteration is of necessity carried into effect by legislators who act under the belief that the change is an amendment; but this law-making opinion is also the opinion of yesterday, because the beliefs which have at last gained such a hold on the legislature as to produce an alteration in the law have generally been created by thinkers or writers,

---

1. *The General Theory*, John Maynard Keynes, Bk. VI, Ch. 24
2. [Macmillan 1952], pp 33-35

who exerted their influence long before the change in the law took place. Thus it may well happen that an innovation is carried through at a time when the teachers who supplied the arguments in its favour are in their graves, or even - and this is well worth noting - when in the world of speculation a movement has already set in against ideas which are exerting their full effect in the world of action and of legislation...

Nor is there anything mysterious about the way in which the thought or sentiment of yesterday governs the legislation or the politics of today. Law-making in England is the work of men well advanced in life; the politicians who guide the House of Commons, to say nothing of the peers who lead the House of Lords, are few of them below thirty, and most of them are above forty years of age. They have formed or picked up their convictions, and, what is of more consequence, their prepossessions, in early manhood, which is the one period of life when men are easily impressed by new ideas. Hence English legislators retain the prejudices or modes of thinking which they acquired in their youth; and when, late in life, they take a share in actual legislation, they legislate in accordance with the doctrines which were current, either generally or in the society to which the law-givers belonged, in the days of their early manhood.

At university they pick up these ideas and then, some twenty five or thirty years later, when they come to the 'levers of power', such ideas are put into effect. Usually these political programmes are the result of the work of an academic who is an individualist or a collectivist, working against the grain of the time, but perhaps living long enough to see his theories realised in the next generation. F A Hayek was an old man before he could safely return to the London School of Economics, without being assailed for his free market vision!

Of course, there are levels of theories, opinions and beliefs at work in society at any given time. The ones we have been describing are relatively short-term, varying with a new generation. Other ideas come down in history, from the influences of such as Locke and Bentham, to the millennial concepts of Christianity. At the present time we participate in the Western Renaissance culture, emanating from Florence in the fifteenth century, with its emphasis on the analytical. If the medieval world can be summarised as believing that Man existed in the body of God; the modern culture is surely, in its origin, the search for God in Man, or in the infinitesimal – the atom, the speck of dust. As William Blake said:

> To see a world in a grain of sand
> And a heaven in a wild flower,
> Hold infinity in the palm of your hand
> And eternity in an hour.

A prime minister and his cabinet, then, find themselves swept forward on a tide of theory, opinion and belief, for which they themselves might not be responsible. There is little opportunity to reconsider or to step back and review the situation. Events are dealt with according to political theory – although sometimes the unexpected, such as war or a natural disaster, breaks through the dream and has to be met with unpremeditated action. An American president is quite frequently challenged by foreign events to devote much of his time away from domestic political pressures; and his responses to these foreign affairs dictate both how he is seen as a world leader and as a re-electable figure in his own country. Either way there is precious little time to reflect on the future of the nation.

This is precisely where a modern, constitutional monarchy is so important. Modern monarchy is creative. It offers continuity and freedom from the current political drag-net, enabling the incumbent or his or her heir to influence, for the good, the future paths of the state. It can rise above the past - which is so often the regulator of government - recognise what is truly happening in the present, and shape the future. In most monarchies there is a requirement to act as guardian of the constitution: perhaps even to step in where the rule of law is challenged, as happened in Australia in 1975, with the Governor-General having to dismiss the prime minister, Gough Whitlam, and his ministers for policies which had polarised opinion throughout the country, bringing it to the verge of civil war. But in the ordinary course of events monarchy does not intervene in current politics, relying on its watchfulness to see that things do not get out of hand, obedient to Bagehot's three rights – the right to be consulted, the right to encourage, the right to warn.[1] 'And', Bagehot goes on to say, 'a king of great sense and sagacity would want no others. He would find that his having no others would enable him to use these with singular effect. He would say to his minister: "The responsibility of these measures is upon you. Whatever you think best must be done. Whatever you think best shall have my full and effectual support. *But* you will observe that for this reason and that reason what you propose to do is bad; for this reason and that reason what you do not propose is better. I do not oppose, it is my duty not to oppose; but observe that I *warn*." Supposing the king to be right, and to have what kings often have, the gift of effectual expression, he could not help moving his minister. He might not always turn his course, but he would always trouble his mind'.

But Bagehot failed to discern that there was a much greater aspect to monarchy: its ability to shape the future. He might have discerned it from the life and work of Albert, the Prince Consort, but did not. Since Bagehot has become the bible of British monarchy, this aspect does not get the attention it deserves.

The Queen has memorably described her role as not doing, but being.[2] She is most perceptive, wise. The centre of a hub of a wheel is stillness. The stillness, the being, the consciousness are requisites for the activity - political and otherwise - which spring from the centre. The Queen in Parliament is sovereign; but also she is Queen in Law and in Council (the executive). It used to be the case that the writ commencing an action in the High Court bore the names of the conflicting parties, but also the name of the

---

1. *The English Constitution*, Vol. V, Collected Works [Economist 1974], p. 253
2. *Elizabeth R*, Antony Jay [BBC Books 1992], p. 236

Queen – 'Elizabeth the Second... WE COMMAND YOU [to] cause an appearance to be entered for you in an action at the suit of –'. The Queen (and, more particularly, the Queen's Judges) was the third point, by reference to whom the disagreement might be resolved. No longer. The old form of writ has disappeared, in favour of a document which baldly states the names of the conflicting parties. Her Majesty has been ignored, as she has been in so many other ways: excluded from postage stamps, where she has become a blob in the background; from the jury oath, where the juror once recited that he would 'well and truly try the several issues joined between our Sovereign Lady the Queen and the defendant' (now rephrased to 'well and truly try the defendant', which is a mere duality between the jury and defendant). She is missing from the proposed new police oath. Her royal train has been taken from her, as indeed has her royal yacht – another example of short-sightedness. What foreign businessman or politician could fail to be impressed by *Britannia* lit up at night, with the Royal Marines marching and counter-marching to their band, and the glitter of diamonds on the bridge?

The Queen stands for self-respect: respect for ourselves as members of an historic nation. Sovereignty is to do with self-respect, as we shall see. Sovereignty pervades the process of coronation. If we do not respect ourselves, then we lose sovereignty, the ability to rule ourselves. But in so many ways the modern political process is to tear down, to reduce, to denigrate our role in the world. This process necessarily begins with our attitude to monarchy. Monarchy symbolises us; and if we denigrate the monarch we denigrate ourselves. Calls to change the Coronation Service, make it less embarrassing to dress up for the occasion, or for the state opening of Parliament, are just attempts to destroy our own self-confidence.

This mocking of the monarchy goes on with regard to its great purpose, which is the long-term care of the nation. Here the Prince of Wales takes an active role, much as his forefather, the Prince Consort, did in Victorian times. Like Albert, the Prince Consort, the Prince of Wales must at times find it a thankless task. Yet he has the courage to persevere in what is undoubtedly his duty - which is to be more outspoken than the Queen - to work for the long-term good of the country. Derision subsides as the truth of what the Prince says, and does, becomes evident to the people, if not to the chattering classes.

Examples from the Prince's Speeches

The Prince operates through words, of course. There is no other way. But coming from such a source, the words are most influential. They are directed to many different sections of society. In an address to the British Medical Association[1] on unorthodox medicine, he said:

> By concentrating on smaller and smaller fragments of the body modern medicine perhaps loses sight of the patient as a whole human being, and by reducing health to mechanical functioning it is no longer able to deal with the phenomenon of healing... The term 'healer' is viewed with suspicion and the concepts of health and healing are probably not generally discussed enough in medical schools. But to reincorporate the notion of healing into the practice of medicine does not necessarily mean that medical science will have to be less scientific.

To the Royal Institute of British Architects he said:[2]

> Now, moreover, we are seeing the gradual expansion of housing co-operatives, particularly in the inner city areas of Liverpool, where the tenants are able to work with an architect of their own who listens to their comments and their ideas and tries to design the kind of environment they want, rather than the kind which tends to be imposed upon them without any degree of choice.

1. 14/12/82. References to speeches are taken from *The People's Prince* [Veritas Publishing, Australia]; the only publisher brave enough to print them!
2. 30/5/84

He could be scathing towards planners and developers:[1]

> Not only did they wreck the London skyline in general. They all did their best to lose the great dome [of St Paul's] in a jostling scrum of office buildings, so mediocre that the only way you ever remember them is by the frustration they induce – like a basketball team standing shoulder-to-shoulder between you and the Mona Lisa.

The English language and its tradition have always been of immense importance to the Prince of Wales, as well as the teaching of it, and the possibilities of a fuller life from reading the best of its literature, including the wealth of the King James Bible and the Prayer Book:[2]

> ...if you actually stand up and talk about the importance of our heritage and the lessons to be learned from our forebears you are at once accused of having a quaint nostalgia for a picturesque, irrelevant past. It has forced me to reflect on why there is such a fierce obsession about being 'modern'. The fear of being considered old-fashioned seems to be so all-powerful that the more eternal values and principles which run like a thread through the whole tapestry of human existence are abandoned under the false assumption that they restrict progress. Well, I'm not afraid of being considered old-fashioned...

> It saddens me, as no doubt it saddens some of you, that we gather to praise Cranmer's great work at a time when it has been battered and deformed in the unlikely cause of making it easier to understand. We seem to have forgotten that for solemn occasions we need exceptional and solemn language: something which transcends our everyday speech. We commend the 'beauty of holiness' yet we forget the holiness of beauty. If we encourage the use of mean, trite, ordinary language we encourage a mean, trite and ordinary view of the world we inhabit.

At the Annual Shakespeare Birthday lecture:[3]

> Many 'ordinary' parents, I suspect, would agree that education is not about social engineering, but about preparing our children as best we can

---

1. Corporation of London, 1/12/87
2. At the presentation of the Thomas Cranmer Schools Prize, 19/12/89
3. 22/4/91

for all the challenges in front of them. This means not only training them for work through the acquisition of knowledge, but also giving them an understanding of themselves and of the deeper meaning of life...

Shakespeare holds up a mirror for us to see ourselves and to experience ourselves, so that we gain in the process a more profound understanding of ourselves and others, appreciating right and wrong, and the factors which make us behave as we do...

Despite all the dramatic changes that have been wrought by science and technology, and the remarkable benefits they have brought us, there remains deep in the soul of each of us, I believe, a vital metaphysical ingredient which makes life worth living. This awareness of a spiritual dimension greater than, and beyond, the confines of our everyday self, and of a purely superficial perception of the physical world in which we exist, has a particular link to aesthetic experience, and to literature...

I don't want my children - or anybody else's - to be deprived of Shake-speare, or of the other life-enhancing elements which I have suggested should be part of the schooling entitlement of all the children of this country... But I fear that these are real dangers if we evade those key questions about the nature and purpose of education which I have touched on today, and if we fail to give our schools and our teachers the resources, and the philosophical framework, they need to produce the right results.

To the Royal College of Psychiatrists:[1]

I do not expect you to agree with me, but I believe that the most urgent need for western man is to rediscover that divine element in his being, without which there can never be any possible hope or meaning to our existence in the earthly realm.

The Prince explains what organic farming means to him:[2]

In farming as in gardening, I believe that if you treat the land with love and respect, it will repay you in kind... Farming has a cultural signifi-cance which distinguishes it from any other activity. It is a way of life

1. 5/7/91
2. as quoted in *Breaking the Cycle,* James Morton [Ebury Press 1998], p. 122

that is, or should be, intimately associated with the long-term health of the soil... I see it as a means by which we can rediscover the rashly abandoned traditional principles which, for thousands of years, have helped to preserve the health and fertility of the soil and the essential diversity of species on which we ultimately depend...

Many might say, 'Fine words; but where are the deeds?' They could be referred to the proliferation of trusts and charities which the Prince has helped to establish, with their emphasis on the future of young people in this country. In a recently published book,[1] James Morton listed some of the achievements since 1972, through the Prince's Trust, Business in the Community and other organizations:

- setting up a self-employment scheme which has started 39,000 businesses and created 52,000 jobs;
- helping over 60,000 other young people to find work;
- enabling nearly 30,000 young people to perform service of benefit both to themselves and their communities;
- pioneering an out-of-school hours programme, Study Support, for over 100,000 students to do homework in conducive surroundings with help at hand;
- encouraging over 400 of the largest companies in Britain to contribute to the regeneration of depressed communities;
- improving the quality of life for disabled people in access, education, employment and healthcare.

Morton adds: 'His work has brought tangible improvement to the lives of over 600,000 disadvantaged young people and in the process generated benefits for the country with a value approaching £12 billion... The institution of monarchy provides [the Prince's] family with an opportunity to think within a time scale which may seem irrelevant to everyday life but could matter a

---

1.   *Ibid.*, Introduction.

great deal to our grandchildren. He has a vision for the country he would like Britain to be today and also far into the future.'

* * * *

The monarch is head of state – which means that the whole panoply of the modern state, not just that part of it administered by Whitehall and Westminster, comes within his or her surveillance. Although seemingly fettered by the will and wishes of a prime minister, the Queen and other members of the royal family are actually free to move about and make contact with people in all walks of life. This they do through visits, appearances at functions, ceremonies in which honours are bestowed, through charities, and through social occasions bringing together a wide variety of people. One should never belittle this contact. The Prime Minister may advise on who is to be knighted, but it is the Queen who actually meets them. Those who are invited to meet the Queen are conscious of a radiance and a majesty which both sustain and exalt them. They are in the presence of something spiritual in the life of their society. When one addresses the question of power within the state, it must never be forgotten that it is this royal influence which can get things done.

Frank Prochaska ended his valuable book, on *Royal Bounty*,[1] with these words:

> Britain's philanthropic traditions, so instrumental in civic life and liberty, are profound. The crown's contribution to these traditions has been and continues to be enabling. The abolition of the monarchy, whatever the benefits, would mark another stage in the perfection of the state monolith. Moreover, it would eliminate that part of the constitution that serves as a buffer between the state and society. It could be argued that this is a role which an elected president could not sustain nor endure. To be sure, the United States has a vibrant voluntary sector without a monarchy, but it has developed its own charitable customs within a quite different

---

1. [Yale 1995], p. 282

social, fiscal and constitutional context. The first lady, however many her charities, cannot be compared to the Queen as a focus of civil society.

It would, however, be wrong to attribute spiritual significance solely to the presence of a crowned monarch. It can happen with an elected American president as well, as Michael Novak explains in the following passage:[1]

> Hands are stretched toward him over wire fences at airports like hands extended to medieval sovereigns or ancient prophets. One wonders what mystic participation our presidents convey, what witness from what other worlds, what form of cure or heightened life. The president arouses waves of 'power', 'being', 'superior reality', as if where he is is history... His office is, in quite modern and sophisticated form, a religion in a secular state. It evokes responses familiar in all the ancient religions of the world. It fills a perennial vacuum at the heart of human expectations.

But how traumatic to find that your President is highly unworthy of your reverence and regard, as happened with Nixon, with Clinton, and with Mitterand in France! Nixon was saved from punishment for his misdeeds by pardon from the incoming President, Gerald Ford, which cost Ford the next election. If there is a law in these matters - as indeed this book proclaims; there is no 'personal immunity' for any ruler - then if the individual escapes punishment the society must pay the price. One wonders how many times the United States will have to suffer the moral confusion, uncertainty and loss of leadership entailed by exonerating corrupt Presidents, before the lesson is learned and they elect a 'natural aristocrat' to high office, as advocated by Thomas Jefferson:[2]... 'there is a natural aristocracy among men. The grounds of this are virtue and talents... The natural aristocracy I consider as the most precious gift of nature for the instruction, the trusts, and

---

1. as quoted in *The State of the Presidency*, Thomas Cronin, [Little Brown 1975] p. 87.
2. to John Adams in 1813: in Cronin, p. 371

the government of society. May we not even say that that form of government is best which provides most effectually for a pure selection of these natural aristoi into the offices of government?'

At an earlier period, before the signing of the federal Constitution, Alexander Hamilton had high hopes for the presidency:[1]

> The process of election affords a moral certainty, that the office of President will never fall to the lot of any man who is not in an eminent degree endowed with the requisite qualifications. Talents for low intrigue, and the little arts of popularity, may alone suffice to elevate a man to the first honours in a single State; but it will require other talents, and a different kind of merit, to establish him in the esteem and confidence of the whole Union... It will not be too strong to say that there will be a constant probability of seeing the station filled by characters pre-eminent for ability and virtue.

The 'little arts of popularity' have taken over with a vengeance. Such is the circus of election that the result is likely to be an incumbent who will least offend the largest number of special interest groups, rather than someone with the integrity to satisfy Thomas Jefferson's description. And this is happening in the most powerful country in the world, with the second oldest constitution. The grubby misbehaviour of Nixon, and of Clinton, calls out almost for the return of a military man (like Washington or Eisenhower) to the highest executive post in America: for the generals, by and large, have relatively clean characters and are honest.

The powers of a French president in the Fifth Republic also lend themselves to corruption. They are awesome powers indeed, set out in grand and vague phrases in Article 5 of the Constitution:

> The President of the Republic sees that the Constitution is respected, ensures by his arbitration the regular functioning of the organs of government and the continuity of the State. He is the protector of national independence, of territorial integrity, and of respect for agreements within the Community and for treaties.

---

1. *The Federalist*, no. lxviii, 14 March 1788

Who could say, when Mitterand set up his special undercover police force, or engaged in lucrative business conspiracies, that he was acting outside his mandate? There is no court in France to challenge the President, except to try him for treason.

All this is not to say that peculation and corruption do not ever occur in monarchies. Of course they do; but at the highest level in the state they are less likely to occur in modern constitutional kingdoms, where the monarch has inherited his office and does not owe any favours to strong electoral interests; where he or she is usually wealthy enough to avoid having to depend on tainted money; and where the monarch can exercise supervision and restraint over the ambitions of unscrupulous ministers. It was very largely the outrage of King George V which forced Lloyd George to appoint a Royal Commission in the early 1920's to advise on the appointment of honours, a system which had been abused by Lloyd George himself to line his own and his party's pockets. Subsequently an Honours (Prevention of Abuses) Act was passed imposing penalties both on those who promised to secure honours in return for payment and on those who promised payment in return for honours.

The contrast in governments in the world today is increasingly between strong, executive presidencies and constitutional monarchies. Wherever one looks, it is the autocrat at the top of so-called 'democratic republics' with whom one has to deal: and in some cases, such as Milosevic in Yugoslavia and Saddam Hussein in Iraq, they carry their people with them as victims of their arrogant ambitions. The rule of constitutional sovereigns is, on the whole, lighter and softer; and their prime ministers not quite as powerful as they might like to be. After all, there can be a succession of prime ministers in one reign, all of whom make their bows and their offerings in the continuous light of the Crown.

Plato, who of all ancient philosophers seems to speak to us today in a way we all understand, argued that moderation was the key to monarchical success: a light hand on the tiller of the state. Elected presidents tend to be heavy-handed, wanting to achieve historical significance for their acts, and knowing they have a limited time in which to prove themselves. An American president, for example, has about a hundred days from initial election to realise his personal goals: after that honeymoon period he is working for re-election, and in the second term of office he is - to mix metaphors - a lame duck.

Influence, rather than direct power, explains the light hand on the tiller of the state. Disraeli, in a public speech at Manchester, in 1872, said:

> I know it will be said that... the personal influence of the Sovereign is now merged in the responsibility of the Minister. I think you will find a great fallacy in this view. The principles of the English Constitution do not contemplate the absence of personal influence on the part of the Sovereign; and if they did, the principles of human nature would prevent the fulfilment of such a theory.

'The principles of human nature' were certainly at work in King Edward VII's reign, when, in 1903, 'dropping in' on the French in Paris, and speaking in fluent French, he won them over with his very presence; thus initiating the process of *entente cordiale*, later extended to the triple entente with France and Russia. A similar result might be said to have occurred when his grandson, that diffident but conscientious King, George VI, visited President Roosevelt in 1939 - 'dropped in' on Hyde Park, the President's home - and had discussions on world affairs which manifestly moved Roosevelt in the direction of supporting Britain in the ensuing conflict.

Often the 'light hand on the tiller' has taken the form of conciliation and moderation. George V was adept at this, having to deal with a number of constitutional crises in his reign: starting with the House of Lords in 1910-11; then in 1914 the Irish Home Rule Bill; and in 1931 the King called together the leaders of the political parties to establish a National Government in the financial crisis of that year. In addition, of course, he and his son had to maintain a high level of morale in the two World Wars. George VI's role in the Second World War was to earn him the Churchillian accolade of a 'spirit undaunted' which gave courage and resolution to his people in the dark days of 1940. The refusal of the royal couple to move out of London, and their frequent visits among bombed-out victims, drew admiration and respect from the population at large.

In a book of that name, *A Spirit Undaunted*,[1] Robert Rhodes James paid tribute to 20th century British monarchs in these words:

> It is often argued that as the ceremonial aspect of the British monarchy has increased immensely in the twentieth century its real influence has diminished – a reflection of Britain's drastically changed position in the world from imperial power to European offshore island. What has really happened is that, with one exception, the occupants of the British throne since the accession of William IV have skilfully accommodated themselves to changing realities. There have been some dark moments. Mistakes have been made. There have been surges of criticism, reasonable or otherwise. Nonetheless, after centuries of turmoil and social and political revolution, the creation and then the loss of a vast Empire, two terrible and near-disastrous world wars, the grievous reduction of wealth and position, and their laborious re-creation, Britain and the British monarchy have survived. And this great achievement was not accidental. Triumphs of character, national and personal, never are.

Monarchs have time on their side, and a family to carry forward their good works. Education within a continuous family is important here: monarchs are trained and dedicated, unlike political presidents who arrive at the seat of power with nothing to commend them but their own driving ambition for personal success. In many of the increasingly autocratic and lengthy presidencies we see around us today, there is no sense of continuity with the past,

---

1. [Little, Brown 1998], pp. 345-6

and no real hope for the future, when the tired incumbent finally relinquishes the reins of power. Walter Bagehot wrote:[1]

> The best reason why monarchy is a strong government is, that it is an intelligible government. The mass of mankind understand it, and they hardly anywhere in the world understand any other. It is often said that men are ruled by their imaginations; but it would be truer to say they are governed by the weakness of their imaginations. The nature of a constitution, the action of an assembly, the play of parties, the unseen formation of a guiding opinion, are complex facts, difficult to know and easy to mistake. But the action of a single will, the fiat of a single mind, are easy ideas: anyone can make them out, and no one can ever forget them. When you put before the mass of mankind the question, 'Will you be governed by a king, or will you be governed by a constitution?' the inquiry comes out thus - 'Will you be governed in a way you understand, or will you be governed in a way you do not understand?

A republic is an intellectual thing. No wonder the Romans embraced the concept! And yet their republican constitution was preposterous and unworkable and finally tilted over, into the lap of empire.[2] A monarchy under law is the best form of government, according to Plato, in *The Statesman*. And it is that because it appeals both to the intellect and to the emotions, to the imagination. You can die for 'King and country'; whereas no one, I think, will ever sacrifice themselves for the President of the European Commission.

In a way, although it is to be regretted that, in the United Kingdom, children are not taught their constitution, there is recognition that such instruction is likely to be dry and unappealing; whereas show them a royal coach, with the Queen inside, wearing a crown, accompanied by an escort of Household Cavalry, and you achieve all that is *essential* in appreciating government. Hence the importance of the Coronation Service which stirs the imagination.

---

1. *English Constitution*, op. cit., p. 226
2. see Finer, *History of Government* [OUP 1997], Vol. I, *Roman Republic*

3

Sovereignty

The concerns of government are broadly threefold: first, sovereignty, then justice, then peace. These provide the conditions in which the life of the community can go on, with the minimum of interference from a central authority. In truth government cannot educate; is not capable of providing medical care; does not know how to make cars; is a failure as an artist. When the Bolsheviks took over in Russia, the shops remained open, the trams kept running, and *Boris Godunov* was being performed at the Opera. It was some time later that the malignant effects of communist doctrine began to be felt. All governments do, in the end, depend on the ordinary life of the community continuing.

Henry de Bracton (1210-1268), our great medieval lawyer and constitutional scholar, spoke of these three factors:[1]

> Those things which belong to jurisdiction and the peace, and those which are incidental to justice or the peace, pertain to no one except to the crown alone and to the royal dignity; nor can they be separated from the crown, since they constitute the crown itself. For the *esse* of the crown is to exercise justice and judgment and to maintain the peace; and without these the crown could neither subsist nor endure.

Sovereignty is a word which, today, is frequently misunderstood. Often one hears of sovereignty being shared, or pooled. This is not possible: you cannot serve two masters. 'Pooling sovereignty is constitutional nonsense', declared John Laughland in his book *The Tainted Source*[2], 'because sovereignty is absolute'.

---

1. as cited in *Constitutionalism, Ancient & Modern*, McIlwain, [Cornell], p.76
2. [Little, Brown 1997]

This country fought two civil wars over the question of sovereignty – the first, the Wars of the Roses, over which dynasty should reign as monarchs; the second was between King and Parliament as to who should be supreme. With typical English moderation, the result was finally to accommodate both King and Parliament in a sovereignty known as the King-in-Parliament.

Much of the confusion over sovereignty - an especially important issue with the arrival on the scene of the European Union - seems to me to derive from the meanings thrown onto the word. In these circumstances it is good to examine the origin of the word. I believe that origin to lie in the Sanskrit language, the root of so much in our European tongues. There the word is *sva-rajan*, 'self-rule' or 'rule of the Self'. It is most important to recognise the Self that rules, for in Vedic terminology this is the *Atman*, the Soul or the Spirit in Man - what the Prince of Wales calls the 'inner spirit', or divinity.

From this concept arises a beautiful analogy of government, both of the individual and of the state, for the two always reflect each other, as Plato observed. You always get the government you deserve. This analogy is a familiar one of a chariot:[1]

> Self rides in the chariot of the body, intellect the firm-footed charioteer, discursive mind the reins.
> Senses are the horses, objects of desire the roads. When Self is joined to body, mind, sense, none but He enjoys.
> When a man lacks steadiness, unable to control his mind, his senses are unmanageable horses.
> But if he control his mind, a steady man, they are manageable horses.

The analogy is exact, for each of us has a soul which travels with us through life, and remains unchanging and true despite any misadventures in the chariot of the body. Intellect, or reason - 'Sovereign Reason', as Shakespeare calls it - should determine

---

1. *The Ten Principal Upanishads*, Purohit Swami & W B Yeats [Faber 1938], p. 32

direction, with a light touch of the reins. Discursive mind is the active part of mind, the messenger, the interpreter: when it is all over the place, out of control, it is Puck in *Midsummer Night's Dream*; when it is obedient to intellect, it is Ariel in *The Tempest*. Either way it is dependent on the senses, which can either gallop away with us, to our destruction; or remain under control and follow the road to salvation. The Self, which started the journey, was aboard all the time, and finishes where we started. It is never shaken or broken, but continues to watch everything and hold everything in place. The Self is the consciousness in which the whole journey takes place.

The analogy of the chariot is one which Plato uses in *Phaedrus*.[1] It was taken up in the Renaissance and used both as a symbol of the soul being drawn towards heaven and also as a political image of the strength and importance of the prince, entering triumphantly into his domain.[2] For our purposes it remains a valid image: self-rule, or sovereignty, begins with the divine presence, continues through the monarch who, with a light touch on the reins, steers the chariot of state into safe paths; the reins are the Parliament which must ever be sensitive to the needs of the people, the horses, who can be swept by passions or sensibly guided to their own best interests. What that means, of course, is that the people are not sovereign. They are ruled from elsewhere, usually by the theories, opinions and beliefs of the time.

Edmund Burke understood this. He wrote:[3]

> It is not necessary to teach men to thirst after power. But it is very expedient that by moral instruction they should be taught, and by their civil constitutions they should be compelled, to put many restrictions upon the immoderate exercise of it, and the inordinate desire. The best method of obtaining these two great points forms the important, but at

1. Section 253
2. see *Art & Power*, Roy Strong [Boydell 1984].
3. *Appeal from the New to the Old Whigs* [1791]

the same time the difficult problem to the true statesman. He thinks of the place in which political power is to be lodged with no other attention than as it may render the more or the less practicable its salutary restraint and its prudent direction. For this reason, no legislator, at any period of the world, has willingly placed the seat of active power in the hands of the multitude; because there it admits of no control, no regulation, no steady direction whatsoever. The people are the natural control on authority; but to exercise and to control together is contradictory and impossible.

It is true that in most written constitutions lip service is paid to the notion that the people are sovereign. Article 3 of the French (1958) Constitution reads: 'National sovereignty belongs to the people, who exercise it through their representatives and by way of referendum'. The Constitution of the United States of America begins: 'WE THE PEOPLE of the United States, in order to form a more perfect Union, establish Justice, insure domestic Tranquility, provide for the common defence, promote the general Welfare, and secure the Blessings of Liberty to ourselves and our Posterity, do ordain and establish this Constitution for the United States of America'. There is a gruff preamble to the German Federal Constitution of 1949: 'The German People...Conscious of their responsibility before God and men...Have enacted, by virtue of their constituent power, this Basic Law for the Federal Republic of Germany...'

In reality, of course, these fine phrases were penned by men who largely selected themselves to speak for the people. They often had 'agendas' of their own. John Adams, second President of the United States, said 'The Federal Constitution was the work of the commercial people in the seaport towns, of the slave-holding states, of the officers of the Revolutionary Army, and the property holders everywhere' –(these interests) finally secured its adoption in 1789 by a narrow margin.[1]

---

1. Bogart, *Economic History of the American People* NY 1946, p224

Charles Beard, economic historian, came to the conclusion that:[1]

> The movement for the Constitution of the United States was originated and carried through principally by four groups of personalty interests which had been adversely affected under the Articles of Confederation [a loose association after the Revolutionary War]: money, public securities, manufactures, and trade and shipping. The first firm steps toward the formation of the Constitution were taken by a small and active group of men immediately interested through their personal possessions in the outcome of their labors... The Constitution was ratified by a vote of probably not more than one-sixth of the adult males...

There was a need for a strong executive, a President, to subjugate the Indians, to destroy Indian claims to land, and to oversee the orderly settlement of the frontier. It is a far cry from Edmund Burke's perception of the English Constitution:[2]

> ... it is a constitution made by what is ten thousand times better than choice; it is made by the peculiar circumstances, occasions, tempers, dispositions, and moral, civil, and social habitudes of the people, which disclose themselves only in a long space of time. It is a vestment which accommodates itself to the body.

The word 'constitution', in fact, means 'standing together': and it is what brings a people together, what is their nature, rather than a set of rules written on a piece of paper. Constitutions therefore vary naturally: the constitution of France is all 'gain and glory', according to Walter Bagehot; the constitution of this country is to love freedom. But it is 'freedom under law' that is the core of English sovereignty (and maybe *British* sovereignty, if that survives).

The written constitutions - which amount to contracts between rulers and the ruled - are right in one respect: there has to be an

---

1. *An Economic Interpretation of the American Constitution* [Free Press 1935], pp 324-5
2. *Speech on Reform of Representation* [1782]

absolute to which reference must always be made, which is sovereign. In the eighteenth century, among the revolutionary states, it was the concept of 'The People', even if, in fact, the People found themselves at the mercy of a small group of oligarchs. Before that, in medieval times, acknowledgment existed that God was sovereign in worldly affairs, as in spiritual. Absolute authority belonged to God alone.

St Paul said:[1] 'Let every soul be subject unto the higher powers. For there is no power but of God: the powers that be are ordained of God'.

The *Wisdom of Solomon*[2] declares: 'Give ear, ye that rule the people, and glory in the multitude of nations. For power is given you of the Lord, and sovereignty from the Highest, who shall try your works, and search out your counsels'.

'There is and must be', wrote Blackstone, in the first volume of his *Commentaries*, 'in all forms of government a supreme, irresistible, absolute, uncontrolled authority, in which the *jura summi imperii*, or the rights of sovereignty reside'. Historically, in the process of Reformation and Renaissance, belief in God as the supreme authority weakened, yet the need for sovereignty continued and was vested in the Prince, so carefully articulated by Machiavelli. Conveniently there was the dictum of Justinian to support the glamour of absolute authority vested in an individual:[3] 'What pleases the prince has the force of law'. This has the effect of a supreme command in continental European constitutions, whatever the words say about a charter belonging to 'the people'. Once the bloody mess and muddle of the French Revolution was out of the way, the Prince stepped onto the stage in the shape of Napoleon, whose word was law throughout most of the continent.

1. *Romans* 13
2. Chap. 6, vv 2-3
3. *Institutes*, 1.2.6

Indeed, he shaped those words into codes, which still govern the daily lives of millions. It would be right to say that *What pleases the prince has the force of law* is the underlying principle of the European Union in that *what pleases the* **commissioners** *has the force of law.*

In contrast with the above, the keystone of the English constitution (said to be 'unwritten', but found principally in Blackstone's *Commentaries*) is the fundamental law expressed by Bracton in the thirteenth century:[1] 'The King must not be under man but under God and under the law, because law makes the king'.

Bracton expands on the statement:

And that he ought to be under law appears clearly in the analogy of Jesus Christ, whose viceregent on earth he is, for though many ways were open to Him for his ineffable redemption of the human race, the true mercy of God chose this most powerful way to destroy the devil's work, he would use not the power of force but the reason of justice...

How important is this statement to English law and liberty! And how much is the Justinian principle, 'What pleases the prince has the force of law', to be resisted, before it erodes our natural freedom!

Two hundred years after Bracton lived, another judge wrote a treatise on kingship, addressed to the young Prince Edward, son of Henry VI, who was to die tragically at the battle of Tewkesbury, in 1471. This book, said Lord Coke in the seventeenth century, should be 'written in letters of gold'. Sir John Fortescue, the author, Chief Justice under Henry, appears in the book, whose Latin title translates as *In Praise of the Laws of England*, as the Chancellor, instructing the young Prince in the art of kingship. He says:[2]

...The King of England is not able to change the laws of his kingdom at his pleasure, for he rules his people with a government not only regal

---

1. *De Legibus* ed. Thorne [Havard 1968]. Vol. 1, p. 33
2. ed. Chrimes, [Cambridge 1942] p. 25

but political. If he were to preside over them with a power entirely regal, he would be able to change the laws of his realm, and also impose on them tallages and other burdens without consulting them. This is the sort of dominion which the Civil Laws indicate when they state 'What has pleased the prince has the force of law'. But the case is far otherwise with the king who rules his people politically, because he is not able himself to change the laws without the assent of his subjects, nor to burden an unwilling people with strange imposts...

The words of Bracton have echoed down the centuries, whenever there has been a challenge to the rule of law. At the time of James I - a tyrant in the making - Chief Justice Coke stood up to him, courageously, when James asserted he too could declare what the law was, to suit his own purposes. Coke said that the law was the golden met-wand and measure to try the causes of subjects, and which protected the king in safety and peace. James was greatly offended and said that meant he was under the law, which was treason to affirm. Coke replied that Bracton had said, 'The king must be under no man but God and the law'.[1] Nevertheless, in the subsequent reign, a civil war had to be fought to bring the crown under law.

The principle was re-stated at the restoration of Charles II. Then at Nuremberg an American prosecutor used it to show that the German leaders could not flout international law. Lord Denning had to remind an Attorney-General that he was under law, when the Attorney refused to give his reasons to the Court.[2] Perhaps the most famous - and significant - recent example of its effect was the determination by the Supreme Court of the United States that a President could not escape the criminal law, when Richard Nixon sought to withhold tapes of conversations in the White House by reason of 'executive privilege'.[3]

---

1. *12 Coke's Reports* 63
2. *Gouriet v Union of Postal Workers* [1977] 1 AER 718
3. *United States v Nixon* 418 US 683 [1974]

The result is, in this country, that all servants of the Crown are responsible to the law; and the law will bring them down if they exceed their powers. A Secretary of State may even be found guilty of contempt of court.[1] There is no special provision for such officers, be they ministers of the Crown or lowly policemen. The ordinary courts of the land can determine whether they acted validly, under the law. The ordinary citizen has wide freedom from restriction, provided always he observes the duties towards others. The Common Law, which controls the use of the powers of the State, is a law of duties, not rights. On the other hand, a servant of the Crown has only those powers laid down for him by Common Law or statute of Parliament. He is kept within the bounds of law by the courts. If he steps outside those bounds he is *ultra vires* and may be condemned. As Mr Justice Laws said, in *Fewings* [1995] 1 AER 513, 'Public bodies and private persons are both subject to the rule of law... [but] the principles which govern their relationships with the law are wholly different. For private persons, the rule is you may do anything you choose which the law does not prohibit... But for public bodies the rule is the opposite. It is that any action taken must be justified by the positive law... The rule is necessary, in order to protect the people from arbitrary interference by those set in power over them.'

The contrary applies on the continent of Europe, where Napoleonic codes flourish. The ordinary citizen is given only such rights as are decreed by the State: the European Convention on Human Rights and Freedoms (note the plural, as though there can be freedom for some but not for others) is a good example, and one which is being followed in this country, unfortunately. Rights divide men, duties bind them together.

The minister, the prefect, the bureaucrat, all have wide, amorphous powers in France and elsewhere. To contest the exercise of

---

1. *M v Home Office* [1994] 1 AC 377

their powers, one would have to go to special administrative tribunals, manned by the peers of the accused politicians. In any event, the judges of the ordinary courts are civil servants, working their way up the ladder of promotion under a Ministry of Justice. The appointment of judges after long experience at the Bar, to a judiciary which is independent of the state - which is the British system - is not a safeguard recognised in continental jurisdictions.

The contrast could not be sharper than between the jury systems of the two countries. In France, the *cour d'assises* sits with three judges and nine jurors: a majority of 8 to 4 must be reached if the defendant is to be convicted, but that includes the judges. They sit in with the jury. Therefore it takes only five jurors and the three judges to convict. Thus the state ensures that it gets the 'right verdict'. The influence of the judges must often sway the ordinary citizens who sit as jurors. And then, by a simple majority in the jury room, the actual sentence is determined. All this would be unthinkable in an English Crown Court. The English judge has nothing to do with the deliberation of the jury; but he alone determines sentence. *Twelve Angry Men* is not likely to happen in a French court.

The process of criminal investigation in France by a *juge d'instruction* makes it almost certain that, by the time a defendant reaches the *cour d'assises*, his conviction has been established, giving rise to the popular, if mistaken, belief that in France you are guilty until proved innocent. Nevertheless, the hurdles are real enough: there is no examination and cross-examination by independent barristers. All questions have to be addressed by or through the judges. Nor is there the painstaking endeavour to exclude potentially prejudicial evidence.

Examples of Common Law Freedom

Civil freedom in Britain has been gained over the centuries, mostly by the efforts of judges. Their foundation was laid for them by Chapter 39 of Magna Carta:[1]

> No freeman shall be arrested, or detained in prison, or deprived of his freehold, or outlawed, or banished, or in any way molested; and we will not set forth against him, nor send against him, unless by the lawful judgment of his peers and by the law of the land.

In *Bushell's Case*[2] a juryman had been fined and imprisoned when he returned a verdict of not guilty, contrary to the opinion of the judge. On a writ of *habeas corpus* Chief Justice Vaughan said:

> How then comes it to pass that two persons [the judge and the juryman] may not apprehend with reason and honesty what a witness, or many, say, to prove in the understanding of one plainly one thing, but in the apprehension of the other, clearly the contrary thing? Must therefore one of these merit fine and imprisonment, because he doth that which he cannot otherwise do, preserving his oath and integrity? And this is often the case of the judge and jury... I conclude therefore that this return... is no cause of fine or imprisonment...

[In other words, any juryman can have an opinion of the case which differs from that of the judge. There is no cause to punish him].

The next case, *Ashby v White and Others*,[3] is very important in English law for establishing the principle, 'Where there is wrong, there is a remedy' (*ubi jus, ibi remedium*). Ashby had been refused a vote in a parliamentary election. The House of Commons asserted that it alone could determine whether the vote had been rightfully refused. Chief Justice Holt, however, took jurisdiction and found for Ashby:

> This is a noble Franchise and Right, which entitles the subject to a share of Government and Legislature. And here the Plaintiff having this Right, it is apparent that the Officer did exclude him from the enjoyment of it, wherein none will say he has done well, but Wrong to the Plaintiff,

---

1. see *Magna Carta* McKechnie [Maclehose 1905] pp 436-7
2. 1670 VI State Trials 999
3. 1704 XIV State Trials 695

and it is not at all material whether the candidate, that he would have voted so, were chosen, or likely to be so, for the Plaintiff's right is the same, and being hindered of that, he has injury done him, for which he ought to have a remedy. It is a vain Thing to imagine, there should be a Right without a Remedy; for Want of Right and Want of Remedy are Convertibles... though the matter be Parliamentary we must not be deterred, but are bound by our Oaths to determine it. The Law consists not in particular Instances, but in the Reason that rules them...

In one famous case, in 1765, the principle was established that a general warrant from a government minister to search some-one's house for possibly seditious material was *ultra vires*: a search warrant had to be specific as to person and property. Lord Chief Justice Camden:[1]

By the Laws of England, every invasion of private property, be it ever so minute, is a trespass. No man can set his foot on my ground without a licence, but he is liable to an action, though the damage be nothing... According to this reasoning, it is now incumbent upon the defendants to show the law by which this seizure is warranted. If that cannot be done it is a trespass...

Somersett's Case[2] is almost too well known to be cited as a case concerning freedom. The words attributed to Lord Mansfield that 'the air of England is too pure for a slave to breathe' were, in fact, those of a barrister in the case. Somersett was a slave who escaped from a ship waiting to take him to Jamaica. The writ of *habeas corpus* ['let us have his body before the court'] has long been a Common Law instrument for doing justice:

[Lord Mansfield said:] The state of slavery is of such a nature, that it is incapable of being introduced on any reasons, moral or political, but only by positive law... It is so odious that nothing can be suffered to support it, but positive law [ie. statute law]. Whatever inconveniences, therefore, may follow from this decision, I cannot say this case is

---

1. *Entick v Carrington* XIX State Trials 1044
2. 1771-2 XX State Trials 1

allowed or approved by the law of England; and therefore the black must be discharged.

Lord Mansfield (1705-93) was an outstanding judge, and a great man. In *The Case of the Dean of St Asaph*[1] he made observations on the freedom of the press and of the judiciary:

> ...It is the duty of the judge, in all cases of general justice, to tell the jury how to do right, though they have it in their power to do wrong, which is entirely a matter between God and their consciences. To be free is to live under a government by law. The liberty of the press consists in printing without previous licence, subject to the consequences of law... The judges are totally independent of the minister that may happen to be, and of the king himself...

In *Wason v Walter*[2] Walter was the publisher of *The Times*. He had published a report of proceedings in Parliament in which, it was alleged, Wason had been defamed. The debate was privileged but, it was claimed, the published report was not. Lord Chief Justice Cockburn:

> Whatever disadvantages attach to a system of unwritten law, and of these we are fully sensible, it has at least this advantage, that its elasticity enables those who administer it to adapt it to the varying conditions of society, and to the requirements and habits of the age in which we live, so as to avoid the inconsistencies and injustice which arise when the law is no longer in harmony with the wants and usages and interests of the generation in which it is immediately applied... Independently of the orders of the houses [of parliament] there is nothing unlawful in publishing reports of parliamentary proceedings. Practically such publication is sanctioned by Parliament; it is essential to the working of our parliamentary system, and to the welfare of the nation.

The greatest judge of this century (even excepting Lord Denning) was the Welsh judge, Lord Atkin, who, in the famous case of *Liversidge v Anderson*,[3] dissented from the majority view in the

---

1. 1783-4 XXI State Trials 847
2. 1868 IV QBD 82
3. [1942] AC 206

House of Lords that the Home Secretary could detain someone under the wartime emergency rules and not give reasons for the detention, despite the regulation stating 'If the Secretary of State has reasonable cause to believe any person to be of hostile origin or associations…' His dissent was subsequently vindicated and is now the law:

> …In this country, amid the clash of arms, the laws are not silent. They may be changed, but they speak the same language in war as in peace. It has always been one of the pillars of freedom, one of the principles of liberty for which on recent authority we are now fighting, that the judges are no respecters of persons and stand between the subject and any attempted encroachments on his liberty by the executive, alert to see that any coercive action is justified in law…

> I protest, even if I do it alone, against a strained construction put on words with the effect of giving an uncontrolled power of imprisonment to the minister… I know of only one authority which might justify the suggested method of construction: "When I use a word", Humpty Dumpty said in a rather scornful tone, "it means what I choose it mean, neither more or less". "The question is", said Alice, "whether you can make words mean so many different things". "The question is", said Humpty Dumpty, "which is to be master – that's all". After all this long discussion the question is whether the words "If a man has" can mean "If a man thinks he has". I am of opinion that they cannot, and that the case should be decided accordingly.

It is a remarkable example of the way in which words can be used to establish freedom. And the freedom also exists for the Common Law judge to express the law in simple terms: one cannot imagine a French or German judge quoting from *Through the Looking Glass*!

Lord Simonds spoke in the House of Lords in the case of *Christie v Leachinsky*.[1] Leachinsky was arrested by two Liverpool detectives who suspected him of theft. They did not inform him at the time of arrest of their suspicion:

---

1. [1947] AC 573

...the arrested man is entitled to be told what is the act for which he is arrested. The 'charge' ultimately made will depend on the view taken by the law of his act... My Lords, the liberty of the subject and the convenience of the police or any other executive authority are not to be weighed in the scales against each other. This case will have served a useful purpose if it enables your Lordships once more to proclaim that a man is not to be deprived of his liberty except in due course and process of law.

The principle of law which is often cited in legal shorthand as *Wednesbury unreasonableness* arose from an important case, decided in 1948, in which Lord Greene, MR, expressed the Common Law powers of a court to restrain activities of government which were plainly unreasonable:[1]

> ... I will summarize once again the principle applicable. The court is entitled to investigate the action of the local authority with a view to seeing whether they have taken into account matters which they ought not to take into account, or, conversely, have refused to take into account matters which they ought to take into account. Once that question is answered in favour of the local authority, it may still be possible to say that, although the local authority have kept within the four corners of the matters which they ought to consider, they have nevertheless come to a conclusion so unreasonable that no reasonable authority could ever have come to it. In such a case, again, I think the court can interfere. The power of the court to interfere in each case is not as an appellate authority to override a decision of the local authority, but as a judicial authority which is concerned, and concerned only, to see whether the local authority have contravened the law by acting in excess of the powers which Parliament confided to them.

* * * *

In these brief quotations from Common Law cases we are reading about the essence of our sovereignty, freedom under law – in fact, the words of judges that give freedom. Law is manifested though speech. Not only that, but there is one voice behind these statements of law: it is a *kind* voice, and one which expresses *fair-*

---

1. *Associated Provincial v Wednesbury Corp.* [1948] 1 KB 223

ness. No wonder that abused peoples, brought relief by invasion, rush towards the tanks and personnel carriers when they hear English being spoken! In so much of the world the voice of the regime is harsh.

McCallum Scott's diary for March 1917 contains the entry:[1]

> As we were leaving the House of Commons last night, he [Winston Churchill] called me into the Chamber to take a last look round. All was darkness except a ring of faint light all around under the Gallery. We could dimly see the Table but walls and roof were invisible. 'Look at it', he said. 'This little place is what makes the difference between us and Germany. It is in virtue of this that we shall muddle through to success and for lack of this Germany's brilliant efficiency leads her to final destruction. This little room is the shrine of the world's liberties'.

And so, may it be said, are the Royal Courts of Justice, administering the Common Law, the law of reason. The judges there are the Queen's Judges, the royal judges, inheritors of the role given them by Henry II in 1179:

> The bishops, earls and magnates of the realm being assembled at Windsor, the king by their common counsel... divided England into four parts. For each part he appointed wise men from his kingdom and sent them through the regions of the kingdom assigned to them to execute justice among the people... Thus he took care to provide for men's needs by setting apart from the generality of mankind those who, albeit they live among men and watch over them, yet possess qualities of insight and boldness superior to those of an ordinary man.[2]

These royal judges swear an oath of allegiance: 'I... do swear that I will well and truly serve our Sovereign Lady Queen Elizabeth... and I will do right to all manner of people after the laws and usages of this realm, without fear or favour, affection or ill-will. So help me God'.[3]

---

1. as quoted in *Muddling Through*, Peter Hennessy [Gollancz 1996], opp. Contents page.
2. *English Historical Documents* Vol. II, pp 480-1
3. ss 4 and 10 Promissory Oaths Act 1868

As they are royal judges, and stand in place of the Queen when giving judgment, so the form of this oath lies at the root of the monarch's status: it is the Royal Law which creates a King or a Queen, as expressed in the Coronation Service, and in the words of Bracton: 'The king must not be under man but under God and the law, for the law makes the king'. 'To do right to all manner of people', and, in particular, 'after the laws and usages of this realm' is the law governing the conduct of Her Majesty. 'The Queen can do no wrong' is a frequently quoted maxim, indicating that the Queen is somehow immune from the law; but one hardly ever hears the corollary being spoken, 'the Queen can only do right'.

In the Coronation Service, the Bible is presented to the monarch with the words, 'Here is Wisdom; This is the royal Law; These are the lively Oracles of God'. And if one searches the references to the kings of Israel, in the Old Testament, one finds constantly the assertion that a particular king 'did that which was right in the sight of the Lord'.[1] It would seem to be a basic requirement of kingship.

But what does it mean, 'to do right to all manner of people after the laws and usages of this realm'? In the first place it means that the monarch, and all her officers, secretaries of state included, must obey the pre-existing law of the courts and of Parliament – obedience exemplified for them by the humility of Alfred, the one king the English call 'Great':

> Then I, King Alfred, collected these [laws] together and ordered to be written many of them which our forefathers observed, those which I liked; and many of those which I do not like, I rejected with the advice of my counsellors, and ordered them to be differently observed. For I dared not presume to set in writing at all many of my own, because it was unknown to me what would please those who should come after us. But those which I found anywhere, which seemed to me most just... I

---

1. see *Cruden's Concordance*, under 'right', especially refs. to Deuteronomy, Kings and Chronicles.

collected herein, and omitted the others. Then I, Alfred, King of the West Saxons, showed these to all my counsellors, and then they said that they were all pleased to observe them.[1]

There are some academics who would say, of the twentieth century monarchy, that it enjoys privileges which put it outside the law. These privileges include: freedom from arrest; freedom from having goods seized; not giving evidence in the monarch's own cause; and, it is even suggested, selective choice of taxation.[2] But the question should rather be, what would be the *result* if the Queen were to behave in a criminal or grossly negligent way? The result, given the massive publicity it would attract, would almost certainly be abdication. For offending against the then law of marriage, as it pertained to the Crown - that the Church could not condone marriage to a twice-divorced woman and the Church was part of the State - Edward VIII had no choice but to abdicate.

J M Jacob argued:[3] '... at the heart of Britain, law does not rule. The Crown is at this centre. If there are laws they are not justiciable in any ordinary sense...'. This is not true, even in the personal sense of the supposed immunity of the Queen, as stated above. Should she - Heaven forbid! - transgress the laws, the penalty is indeed heavy. However, it is more likely that it is the royal exemption from personal taxation, as from time to time practised, that causes envy, and the meanness towards public office which characterises this country. 'There is, in fact', wrote George Trefgarne in *The Spectator*[4], 'a good case for saying that the monarchy does not cost anything at all and that ordinary taxpayers benefit from it. At the beginning of every reign the sovereign hands over about £2 billion of property to the government, known as the Crown Estate... Last year it provided revenue to the government

---

1. *English Historical Documents*, Vol. I, p. 373
2. *The Nature of the Crown* [OUP 1999], chap. 7
3. *The Republican Crown* [Aldershot: Dartmouth 1996] p. 1
4. 20 March 1999, p. 56

of £113 million. The costs of the monarchy [about £40 million] are thus more than met by the Crown Estate, with the balance left for general government spending'. None of this, of course, rates a mention in the press, as it continues its campaign of denigration.

Maurice Ashley, in his book *The Glorious Revolution of 1688*[1], cites Sir Edward Coke, the eminent 17th century judge, as an advocate of the view that the King was subject to the immemorial laws of the English people – a view supported by Holdsworth who also reports that Coke held that judges must impartially expound and apply a supreme law to which the Crown was as much subject as any other citizen.[2]

This 'supreme law' is, of course, the Common Law, which is the natural law of the English-speaking peoples. Statute law - the law made by Parliament - may affect or alter the Common Law for a time; but we always revert to the principles of the Common Law when we seek freedom. 'The stress which [Sir John Fortescue] laid in all his writings upon the supreme importance of the law of God and of nature... was a factor in the transmission to modern times of the concept of a fundamental law to which all other laws must conform'.[3]

> The principle of parliamentary sovereignty therefore implies that the courts will not intrude into the legislative process, and that an Act of Parliament validly passed under the appropriate procedure and in the accustomed form must be put into effect. Its meaning and effect must, however, be examined if any question about them arises in the course of litigation. Here the canons of interpretation followed by the judges embody in an attenuated form the ancient doctrine... that there was a sense in which the common law was fundamental. A statute which is contrary to the reason of the common law or purports to take away a prerogative of the Crown is none the less valid, but it will, so far as is pos-

---

1. [Hodder & Stoughton 1966] Chap. VIII, as cited in *The Nature of the Crown*, op. cit., p. 313
2. W S Holdsworth [1932] 48 LQR 25 at 29
3. HD Hazeltine, Preface to the Chrimes ed. of *De Laudibus*, p. 1

sible, be applied in such a way as to leave the Prerogative or the common law rights of the subject intact. To this extent the reason of the common law still prevails; we cannot say that Parliament cannot do any of these things, but we can still say that there is a presumption against its doing them.[1]

It is the Common Law which gives rise to the second aspect of the rule that the Queen can only do right. That is the prerogative power of the Crown, exercised most broadly by ministers and judges, but whose residual capacity to do right must remain with the monarch. However, it is part of the Common Law and is therefore reviewable by the Courts. 'In every case the King must make good at common law his claim to the prerogative; the mere plea of prerogative no longer ousts the jurisdiction of the court.'[2]

What is the prerogative? Blackstone says:[3]

By the word prerogative we usually understand that special pre-eminence which the king hath, over and above all other persons, and out of the ordinary course of the common law, in right of his regal dignity. It signifies, in its etymology, (from *prae* and *rogo*) something that is required or demanded before, or in preference to, all others. And hence it follows, that it must be in its nature singular and eccentrical; that it can only apply to those rights and capacities which the king enjoys alone, in contradistinction to others, and not to those he enjoys in common with any of his subjects: for if once any one prerogative of the crown could be held in common with the subject, it would cease to be prerogative any longer. And therefore Finch lays it down as a maxim, that the prerogative is that law in case of the king, which is law in no case of the subject.

Bagehot wrote amusingly about the prerogative in his day, the nineteenth century:[4]

---

1. Keir and Lawson, *Cases in Constitutional Law* [Clarendon 1967], p. 9
2. *Ibid.*, p. 101
3. *Commentaries*, op. cit. Vol. 1, Ch. 7
4. *Collected Works*, op. cit. Vol. V, pp 182-3

Not to mention other things, [the Queen] could disband the army (by law she cannot engage more than a certain number of men, but she is not obliged to engage any men); she could dismiss all the officers, from the General Commanding-in-Chief downwards; she could dismiss all the sailors too; she could sell off all our ships of war and all our naval stores; she could make a peace by the sacrifice of Cornwall, and begin a war for the conquest of Brittany. She could make every citizen in the United Kingdom, male or female, a peer; she could make every parish in the United Kingdom a 'university'; she could dismiss most of the civil servants; she could pardon all offenders. In a word, the Queen could by prerogative upset all the action of civil government within the government, could disgrace the nation by a bad war or peace, and could, by disbanding our forces, whether land or sea, leave us defenceless against foreign nations. Why do we not fear that she would do this, or any approach to it?

He tells us that any minister who recommended such drastic action could either be dealt with by way of impeachment, as having treasonable intentions; or, in the modern way, the minister would lose the confidence of Parliament and have to resign. Either way the Queen herself would escape liability; it would be down to her advisers.

In present-day terms, the prerogative might be described, in Dicey's words, as the 'residue of discretionary or arbitrary authority, which at any given time is legally left in the hands of the Crown'.[1] All governments must, of course, possess such authority, largely to act in cases of emergency, so that the powers are, for example, to wage war, or to make peace; to enter into treaties; to protect children who are abused; to curb civil disobedience; to show mercy to, or pardon, offenders. These powers, as has been said, are now largely exercised by ministers or officials, acting under the supervision of Parliament and the Courts. But it is the case that the Queen herself, as guardian of the Constitution, might

---

1. *Introduction to the Law of the Constitution* [MacMillan 1959], p. 424

have to 'do right' by intervening personally. The sovereign, in Carl Schmitt's definition, is the one who takes the decision in exceptional circumstances.[1]

That eventuality is recognised by our leading constitutional experts. Rodney Brazier, in the book *The Nature of the Crown*,[2] says:

> ...if a government were able to persuade Parliament to pass a Bill subversive of the democratic basis of the constitution, the Queen might feel justified in vetoing it in her capacity as the ultimate guardian of the constitution; she could more appropriately insist, however, on a general election to test the electorate's attitude to the Bill, and leave the question of royal assent until that verdict was available. Vigorous private protest, perhaps followed by a general election forced by the Head of State if the government persisted in its plans, would be a safer royal reaction, for it would throw the final decision to the voters.

Vernon Bogdanor has written:[3]

> ... the sovereign cannot be bound by precedent. He or she will be called upon to do what is best in a specific situation whose precise contours cannot be predicted... Under emergency conditions, the role which the sovereign might adopt could well become controversial. Some would argue that it is in such a situation that the sovereign should be able to exercise his or her prerogative powers as a guarantor of the constitution, a defender of last resort of the conventions of parliamentary government. That was the role adopted by King Juan Carlos of Spain in 1981 when his country was threatened by a military coup.

But there is an example of this final power being used in the English-speaking world, showing how necessary it is in an emergency. In 1975 the Australian Federal Government, socialist and led by Gough Whitlam, had polarised the country into two camps: those who supported its irregular use of funds to finance grandiose

---

1. as quoted in *The Tainted Source*, op. cit., p. 182
2. op. cit., p. 343
3. *The Monarchy and the Constitution* [Clarendon 1995], pp 75, 77-8

schemes; and those who wished to bring the government back under law. The division was clearly marked in the Senate, which had refused its consent to the Budget for the year, thus cutting off funds necessary for paying the normal expenses of government, such as paying the civil servants, the police and armed forces, the teachers, and so on. The Federal Parliament was deadlocked, as was the country at large. Gough Whitlam had acted throughout in a dictatorial manner, expecting the Governor-General, the Queen's representative, to carry out his wishes. In those circumstances the obvious solution to the conflict was for the Prime Minister to call a double election, for the House of Representatives and for the Senate. But he was unwilling to do so, no doubt aware that his high-handed and expensive plans for Australia might not be acceptable to the electorate.

The Governor-General, Sir John Kerr, who had been appointed by the Queen only the year before, on the advice of Mr Whitlam, had to consider what was right for the country. If Whitlam refused to dissolve Parliament, in the face of the obstinacy of the Senate, the situation was serious indeed. Civil conflict might erupt, so bitter was the controversy. Mindful of this, the Governor-General took the advice of the Chief Justice, Sir Garfield Barwick, who wrote as follows:[1]

> In response to Your Excellency's request for my legal advice as to whether a course on which you had determined was consistent with your constitutional authority and duty, I respectfully offer the following.

> The Constitution of Australia is a federal constitution which embodies the principle of ministerial responsibility. The Parliament consists of two houses, the House of Representatives and the Senate, each popularly elected, and each with the same legislative power, with the one exception that the Senate may not originate nor amend a money bill.

> Two relevant constitutional consequences flow from this structure of the Parliament. First, the Senate has constitutional power to refuse to

1. Sir John Kerr, *Matters for Judgment* [MacMillan 1979], pp 342-343

pass a money bill; it has power to refuse supply to the Government of the day. Secondly, a Prime Minister who cannot ensure supply to the Crown, including funds for carrying on the ordinary services of Government, must either advise a general election... or resign. If, being unable to secure supply, he refuses to take either course, Your Excellency has constitutional authority to withdraw his Commission as Prime Minister.

In the words of Sir John Kerr, the story continues, on the 11th November 1975, at the Governor-General's residence:[1] 'When Mr Whitlam entered my study he put his hand into his inside coat pocket and I said to him, "Before you say anything, Prime Minister, I want to say something to you. You have told me this morning on the phone that your talks with the leaders on the other side have failed to produce any change and that things therefore remain the same. You intend to govern without parliamentary supply". He said, "Yes". I replied that in my view he had to have parliamentary supply to govern and as he had failed to obtain it and was not prepared to go to the people, I had decided to withdraw his commission.

'Things then happened as I had foreseen. Mr Whitlam jumped up, looked urgently around the room, looked at the telephones and said sharply, "I must get in touch with the Palace at once" [for the purpose of advising the Queen of Australia to dismiss her Governor-General]. He did not interpret what I had so far said as an actual withdrawal of his commission and indeed it was not. He still had time in which to act; and he made it obvious what his action would be: not to seek to discuss with me any change of attitude, not to seek to go to the people in an election as Prime Minister, but to move at once for my dismissal by so advising the Queen.

'The documents, duly signed, were face downwards on my desk. I now knew there would be no changed advice, only the certainty of constitutional disruption if any time were allowed to elapse. I therefore made my final decision to withdraw his com-

---

1. *Ibid.*, pp 358-9

mission and hand him the signed documents. He could still say, "Let us talk about this. If you are determined to have an election, I would rather go to the people myself, as Prime Minister". Had he done so I would have agreed, provided he committed himself by action there and then. I was not prepared to run any further risks.

'When he said, "I must get in touch with the Palace at once", I replied, "It is too late". He said, "Why?" and I told him, "Because you are no longer Prime Minister. These documents tell you so, and why". I handed them to him and he took them. He did not read them. There was a short silence after which he said, "I see", and stood up. He made no gesture towards discussion. He turned to the door and I came round my desk towards him. I said, "I tried to get a compromise and failed". I waited but he still said nothing. I said, "We shall all have to live with this". Mr Whitlam said, "You certainly will"'.

Later, outside Parliament House, when the proclamation of dissolution was read, Whitlam told his supporters, 'Maintain your rage', thus demonstrating the complete irresponsibility with which he had conducted the affairs of the Commonwealth. A caretaker government was appointed; and at the subsequent General Election, Whitlam and his party were not returned to government. Nevertheless, he and his party saw to it that the Governor-General was vilified.

The following day, the Speaker of the House of Representatives sought to bring the Queen into the dispute. Her Private Secretary wrote back as follows:[1]

> I am commanded by The Queen to acknowledge your letter of 12th November about the recent political events in Australia. You ask that The Queen should act to restore Mr Whitlam to office as Prime Minister.

---

1. *Ibid.*, pp 374-5

As we understand the situation here, the Australian Constitution firmly places the prerogative powers of the Crown in the hands of the Governor-General as the representative of The Queen of Australia. The only person competent to commission an Australian Prime Minister is the Governor-General, and The Queen has no part in the decisions which the Governor-General must take in accordance with the Constitution. Her Majesty, as Queen of Australia, is watching events in Canberra with close interest and attention, but it would not be proper for her to intervene in person in matters which are so clearly placed within the jurisdiction of the Governor-General by the Constitution Act.

The letter is interesting, in that it shows the Queen fulfilling her role of constant watchfulness: 'being' as she describes it, rather than 'doing'. But if it were right to do so, the Queen might, however, have to intervene in person in the government of this country. One hopes that the occasion will not arise: but there are signs of increasingly intolerant party politics causing divisions in the United Kingdom. No one can predict whether these divisions will produce an attack on the 'democratic basis of the constitution'. But if they do, the Queen might have the responsibility of restoring the democratic balance. It would be a hard decision to have to make and would inevitably bring criticism on to the Crown. But the Queen has sworn an oath at her coronation, and she would have to 'do right' in whatever circumstances she has to meet.

4

Coronation

C oronation is the recognition of the importance of religion
to the kingship of a nation. When one refers to the English-
speaking nation, one is talking about a world-wide
phenomenon. And certainly, within that nation, the Christian
religion is pervasive, even if church-going in some parts is slight.
The 'Government of God' is never far away, according to the
statistics; and therefore it is good to have a monarchy, both in
mother country and in the Commonwealth, which reflects that
religious strength. One should also recall the true meaning of
'religion': Skeat, in his great Etymological Dictionary, reminds us
that 'religens' is the opposite of 'negligens', or lack of care.[1]

Bagehot said:[2] '... the English monarchy strengthens our government with the strength of religion. It is not easy to say why it
should be so. Every instructed theologian would say that it was the
duty of a person born under a republic as much to obey that republic as it is the duty of one born under a monarchy to obey the monarch. But the mass of the English people do not think so; they
agree with the oath of allegiance; they say it is their duty to obey
the "Queen"; and they have but hazy notions as to obeying laws
without a queen'.

Taine, in his monumental *History of English Literature*,[3]
paints a sombre picture of the Saxon era that nevertheless

---

1. I am indebted to the late, and sorely missed, language exponent
   Sheila Rosenberg for pointing this out
2. *Works*, op. cit. Vol. V, p. 230
3. [Chatto & Windus 1887], Vol. 1, p. 44

61

implanted the religious inclination of the English race:

> A race so constituted was predisposed to Christianity, by its gloom, its
> aversion to sensual and reckless living, its inclination for the serious and
> sublime... This restlessness, this feeling of the infinite and dark beyond,
> this sober, melancholy eloquence were the harbingers of spiritual life.
> We find nothing like it amongst the nations of the south, naturally
> pagan, and preoccupied with the present life. These utter barbarians
> embrace Christianity straightway, through sheer force of mood and
> clime... They possess the idea of God.

Elsewhere, Taine follows Tacitus in describing features of our
Saxon forebears which are still recognisable today:[1]

> Huge white bodies, cool-blooded, with fierce blue eyes, reddish flaxen
> hair; ravenous stomachs, filled with meat and cheese, heated by strong
> drinks; of a cold temperament, slow to love, home-stayers, prone to
> brutal drunkenness...

There are, however, redeeming features, as Tacitus demon-
strates:[2]

> The power even of the kings is not absolute or arbitrary... On matters of
> minor importance only the chiefs debate; on major affairs the whole com-
> munity. But even where the commons have the decision, the subject is
> considered in advance by the chiefs... such hearing is given to the king
> or state-chief as his age, rank, military distinction or eloquence can secure
> – more because his advice carries weight than because he has the power
> to command. If a proposal displeases them, the people shout their dissent;
> if they approve, they clash their spears. To express approbation with their
> weapons is their most complimentary way of showing agreement.

To the Saxon kings, Alfred in particular, Christianity was of
prime importance in the State, and the king upheld religion. This
is what Wulfstan, author of *Institutes of Polity* said in the tenth
century:[3]

> ...true it is what I say, if Christianity be weakened, the kingdom will

---

1.   *Ibid.*, p. 26
2.   *Germania*, [Penguin Classic 1948], p. 107, pp 110-111
3.   Thorpe, *Ancient Laws* [1840], p. 424

forthwith totter; and if bad laws be set up anywhere in the nation, or vicious habits be anywhere too much loved, that will be all to the nation's detriment: but let be done as it is requisite, let unrighteousness be suppressed, and God's righteousness upraised; that may be beneficial before God, and before the world. Amen.

In such exquisite and simple language, the author describes the function of the king:[1]

It is very rightly the duty of a Christian king to be in the place of a father to a Christian nation, and in watch and in ward Christ's viceregent, so as he is accounted. And it is also his duty, with all his mind, to love Christianity, and shun heathenism, and everywhere to honour and protect God's church, and to establish peace among, and reconcile all Christian people with just law; as he most diligently may; and thereby he shall prosper in good, because he loves justice, and shuns injustice.

This remains a fine description of the function of a king (or queen) even in the modern world, and shows the importance of Christianity to the State. While other religions and beliefs may have their place in the modern society of England especially, it must never be forgotten that the primary influence on our culture, thinking and language is Christian; and the ceremony of coronation is 'intended to be the consecration of the sovereign to a definitely ecclesiastical position, carried out with great stateliness and elaboration... the King is no mere lay person, but is to be regarded as one of the clergy, though at the same time not a priest'.[2]

Such is the importance generally of the Anglo-Saxon *Institutes of Polity* that most of it is reproduced herein, as an appendix. Now that there is a move afoot no longer to teach Anglo-Saxon in our schools and universities, every opportunity should be taken to remind ourselves of the simplicity and beauty of language in this golden age in the life of a most ancient kingdom.

But much older is the statement from one of the Upanishads

---

1.   *Ibid.*, p. 422
2.   *The Coronation Service*, Eeles [Mowbray 1952] pp10-11

of India:[1]

> Hence the king is above all men. The priest occupies a lower seat at the
> coronation. The priest confers the crown upon the king, is the root of the
> king's power.
>
> Therefore though the king attain supremacy at the end of his coronation
> he sits below and acknowledges him as the root of his power. So who-
> ever destroys the priest, destroys his root. He sins; he destroys the good.

This relationship between priest and king is therefore ancient,
going back beyond our biblical history, which itself acknowledges
the importance of the link. Anson, our great constitutional authority, spoke of it in this way:[2]

> The Queen is Head of the Church, not for the purpose of discharging
> any spiritual function, but because the Church is the National Church,
> and as such is built into the fabric of the State. The Crown itself is held
> on condition that the holder should be in communion with the Church
> of England as by law established.

'Built into the fabric of the State'. 'The priest is the root of the
king's power'. Whoever believes that today? More importantly,
does the *Church* believe it? So much of its natural authority is sur-
rendered in its bid ever to remain popular. No one - or very few -
hears its voice today. Yet a great churchman can speak out, and he
will have influence in the affairs of men. One such was Archbishop William Temple, whose voice you could not fail to hear. In
1942, during the worst of the war, Penguin published his *Christianity and Social Order*[3], read by very many people, from all walks
of life. In Chapter IV the Archbishop wrote:

> If Christianity is true at all it is a truth of universal application; all things
> should be done in the Christian spirit and in accordance with Christian
> principles. 'Then', some say, 'produce your Christian solution for

---

1. *Ten Principal Upanishads*, Shree Purohit Swami and W B Yeats
    [Faber 1952], p. 122

2. *Law & Custom of the Constitution* [Oxford 1892]Vol. II, p. 378

3. Reprinted [1987] Shepheard-Walwyn

unemployment'. But there neither is nor could be such a thing. Christian faith does not by itself enable its adherent to foresee how a vast multitude of people, each one partly selfish and partly generous, and an intricate economic mechanism, will in fact be affected by a particular economic or political innovation... 'In that case', says the reformer - or, quite equally, the upholder of the *status quo* - 'keep off the turf. By your own confession you are out of place here'. But this time the Church must say 'No; I cannot tell what is the remedy; but I can tell you that a society of which unemployment (in peace time) is a chronic feature is a diseased society, and that if you are not doing all you can to find and administer the remedy, you are guilty before God'. Sometimes the Church can go further than this and point to features in the social structure itself which are bound to be sources of social evil because they contradict the principles of the Gospel.

So the Church is likely to be attacked from both sides if it does its duty. It will be told that it has become 'political' when in fact it has been careful only to state principles and point to breaches of them; and it will be told by advocates of particular policies that it is futile because it does not support these. If it is faithful to its commission it will ignore both sets of complaints, and continue so far as it can to influence all citizens and permeate all parties.

With what authority the Archbishop speaks! Churchmen now seem to want to cower in their corners, letting all manner of moral and political decline pass without comment. They have cheapened the language of their liturgy; they have condoned lust and avarice; they have kept quiet when what is required by the people is leadership. But it is, on the other hand, a very simple thing if one of them chooses to speak out, to state, as the Archbishop says, principles and point to breaches of them. This is what people want to hear. They need to be inspired. Recently there was a small white statue of Christ placed on a plinth in Trafalgar Square: not only was it small and insignificant, but the features of the face were insipid, vacuous. Of one thing one can be sure: Christ carried with him a natural authority. He walked, talked, sat, acted as a man of steady wisdom. This would have showed in his physical presence. People *wanted* to follow him, and would not have followed a vapid, miserable creature such as was depicted in our premier square.

In the Coronation Service are enunciated principles, in magnificent language. Not the mundane political jargon of the day, nor even the few, sparse words with which an American President makes his oath to the constitution. Here are everlasting Christian principles laid out before us, in a theatre in the centre of an Abbey. 'Principle' means a 'fundamental truth or law, a tenet, a settled rule of action', but also, 'a beginning'. When the Coronation Service utters its powerful declarations of justice, mercy and rule of law it does so at the *beginning* of government. All government stems from these words, however technical and material it may seem to become. Not much can basically go wrong with government as long as these principles are sounded and listened to. There needs to be a constant reminder that these are principles by which to live; and a constant will not to let them be destroyed. 'The priest is the root of the king's power... whoever destroys the priest, destroys his root. He sins; he destroys the good'.

The 'prince' is a word cognate with 'principle'.[1] The Queen embodies these principles of law, justice and mercy; and no one - not even a Prime Minister - can forget it.

But it is always possible that the Coronation Service for a future monarch could be changed, made less 'lavish', more in tune with the modern approach: already there are comments about the Queen's oath to maintain in the United Kingdom the Protestant Reformed Religion (possibly because of the Northern Ireland situation) and maintain and preserve **inviolably** the settlement of the Church of England (which can only mean its function as part of the government of the State). It must be remembered that the Queen has sworn an oath to defend this institution: during her lifetime, at least, there can be no challenge to the authority of the Church of England. The oath is sacred.

---

1. see *Skeat's Etymological Dictionary*, under 'principle'

In fact, although there have been changes, the Coronation Service is much the same as it was in the eighth century.[1] It was practically untouched by the Reformation. The same Latin service was used for Elizabeth I as for Henry VII and Henry VIII. It was translated into English for James I (VI of Scotland). James II, as a Romanist, refused to receive Communion, an essential part of the service. However, it was restored, with the accession of William and Mary in 1689. The Coronation Service, in fact, was inserted in the middle of the Communion Service, in the position it occupied in the earliest order of all – that of Egbert. It has descended through the eighteenth century, was used for the coronation of Queen Victoria in 1838, and the coronations of Edward VII, George V, George VI, and Elizabeth II.

Francis Eeles said:[2]

> It is really wonderful that it survived in such a full and elaborate form as it has. But it must be clearly understood that, setting aside the James II order, which was never used again, the alterations and omissions had little or no doctrinal significance; they were the result of a craze for shortening the service, coupled with ignorance, bad liturgical taste, and great carelessness… As a work of liturgical art, those alterations spoiled it greatly, but they in no way changed its theological character, and they were all omissions of what have never been regarded as essentials in any part of the Church.

The Archbishop of Canterbury introduced the Coronation Service of Queen Elizabeth II with these words: 'The Coronation is the occasion for much splendid pageantry: it would be an empty show without that profound significance which is so dramatically displayed in the Coronation Service. There the Church of the English People, which was the *Ecclesia Anglicana* before there was a nation, acting for all the peoples of Kingdom and Commonwealth, consecrates the Queen, by prayer and sacrament in the name of

---

1.   *The Coronation Service*, Eeles, op. cit.
2.   *Ibid.*, p. 25

God, to her lifelong service'.

Without going into great detail with regard to the splendours of the pageantry, which may be read about in the Service printed as an appendix, let us look at the substance of some of the text used in the Coronation Service. Here we are assisted greatly by the division made by E Christian Ratcliff in his book *The Coronation Service of Her Majesty Queen Elizabeth II*, at p. 34:

(i)   The people accept the Queen as Sovereign at **THE RECOGNITION**;

(ii) The Queen, in taking **THE OATH** makes her solemn promise to govern by and maintain the Laws of her Peoples;

(iii) At **THE ANOINTING** the Queen receives Consecration, or the grace of a special Divine Blessing, for her sovereign office and work;

(iv) **THE INVESTITURE** with **THE SWORD, THE ROYAL ROBE, THE SCEPTRE** and **ROD**, etc., **THE CROWNING**, and **THE INTHRONIZATION** are the outward and visible signs of the Queen's assumption of her royal office.

The Recognition

Following the entry into the Abbey, the instructions say: *The Queen shall in the mean time pass up through the body of the Church, into and through the choir, and so up the stairs to the Theatre; and having passed by her Throne, she shall make her humble adoration, and then kneeling at the faldstool set for her before her Chair of Estate on the south side of the Altar, use some short private prayers; and after, sit down in her Chair.*

'up the stairs to the Theatre' This is a platform set up at the crossing of the transepts, and has steps leading up to it on all sides.

The Queen's Throne is placed on it, facing the Altar. How appropriate that it should be described as the Theatre! The whole ceremony is theatre of the mind of an ancient nation. Here are demonstrated the virtues and values which the nation, ultimately, holds dear to itself and to God. They are spoken and sounded in music, and the clergy and the Queen are vested with the clothes and symbols of a rich imagination. Thus do we celebrate the brilliance of mind and soul, when consecrated to God. It is not a dry, factual approach: it speaks of the rich divinity in all of us. It is also joyous, full of colour and light – incomparably better than the drab inauguration of a president! This is one constitution in the world today that has at its heart a song of praise.

The Archbishop, together with the Lord Chancellor, Lord Great Chamberlain, Lord High Constable, and Earl Marshal (Garter King of Arms preceding them) shall then go to the East side of the Theatre, and after shall go to the other three sides in this order, South, West, and North, and at every of the four sides the Archbishop shall with a loud voice speak to the People; and the Queen in the meanwhile, standing up by King Edward's Chair, shall turn and show herself unto the People at every of the four sides of the Theatre as the Archbishop is at every of them, the Archbishop saying: 'Sirs, I here present unto you the Queen Elizabeth, your undoubted Queen: Wherefore all of you who have come this day to do your homage and service, Are you willing to do the same?'

The People signify their willingness and joy, by loud and repeated acclamations, all with one voice crying out,

GOD SAVE QUEEN ELIZABETH.

Then the trumpets shall sound.

'shall turn and show herself unto the People' This is an election, of very old significance, in which the people give their 'vote' and voice to the incoming monarch. But this 'vote' is far more serious than the occasional marking of a ballot paper; it derives from the word 'vow', meaning a solemn promise. Thus the vow is to follow and serve Queen Elizabeth. Anything which detracts from that service is wrong. It is a breach of a solemn promise. And the Queen herself makes a vow to her peoples, as is evidenced by the next stage, the taking of the Oath.

The Taking of the Oath

This is the most important stage of the coronation; for it is here that the Queen makes her solemn promise of service to her peoples – not only in the United Kingdom, but across the world. Having sworn her oath in such sacred surroundings the oath must be kept; and no Minister anywhere should attempt to put the Queen in a position where the oath is denied.

There is, currently, a view that an oath is a formality, which doesn't matter a great deal in the scheme of things. Jonathan Aitken, an ex-Minister of the Crown, confessed to perjuring himself and attempting to get his daughter to perjure herself, and some people questioned whether it was right to send him to prison for such an offence. But it is a grave offence, because it puts in peril a man's own soul. In a day and age when 'soul' does not seem to mean very much, it is not surprising that people should have a negligent attitude towards oath-taking. However, putting aside the concept of soul, 'truth' is a word which is still cherished by most people; and the public declaration of something as true which is in fact a lie undermines the credibility of the speaker as well as all society, as was recognised only too clearly in the case of Richard Nixon, President of the United States.

Indeed, it was not long ago historically that prisoners charged with murder were not allowed to give evidence in their own behalf because of the temptation to perjure themselves. The soul was to be valued above everything else.

The rot set in, as far as English law is concerned, with the judgment of the Lord Chief Justice in the case brought by the Government against *The Times* newspapers and the literary executors of Richard Crossman, in 1975. The Attorney-General sought injunctions against the publication of Crossman's *Diaries*, because of breaches of confidence in relating discussions which had taken place in Cabinet. As a Cabinet Minister, Richard Crossman had sworn the Privy Councillor's oath, part of which declared: 'You shall, in all things to be moved, treated and debated in Council, faithfully and truly declare your Mind and Opinion according to your Heart and Conscience; and shall keep secret all Matters committed and revealed unto you or that shall be treated of secretly in Council'.

The Lord Chief Justice dismissed this aspect of the case in the following words: 'It seems to me, therefore, that the Attorney-General must first show that whatever obligation of secrecy or discretion attaches to former Cabinet Ministers, that obligation is binding in law *and not merely in morals*'. (Emphasis added). This opinion must be mistaken: the Lord Chief Justice would have had some harsh things to say if one of his Judges had failed to live up to the oath he had sworn on being appointed a Judge. In fact, Sidney Low observed:[1] 'To the Cabinet Councillor the oath is a serious matter. The pledge to maintain secrecy cannot be deemed a mere form. It is not merely the King's secrets that the minister swears to keep, but also, and particularly, the secrets of his colleagues. Under this provision everything which passes at a Cabinet meeting is strictly confidential... As Privy Councillor *the legal offence* he can commit is a failure to observe the terms of his oath, in every particular...' (Emphasis added).

Despite this, the Lord Chief Justice (Lord Widgery) swept aside the considerations of oath-taking and allowed the commercial interests behind the action to succeed, very largely, in cashing

---

1.   *The Governance of England* [Fisher Unwin 1904], pp 31-32

in on Crossman's breaches of confidence. What effect this must have had on later Cabinet meetings, with its members secretly writing down their thoughts on their colleagues, rather than attending to their duties, history alone will tell. But it was a tragic judgment for the Common Law, which is built on truth and reason.

The point is, that there are no contracts of employment at such high levels in the government of the nation. The Queen is not contracted to her people, as she might be if a written constitution were to be introduced. What happens is that she is granted the *status* of sovereign, in return for an oath which requires utmost service from her, all the days of her life. This service is not narrowed down to the four corners of a contract, but is total. The same wide obedience is expected from all those who advise her as Ministers and those who achieve the status of Judges. Status is confirmed by oath and is infinitely better than contract, wherein an attempt is made to define and limit service in exchange for monetary consideration. The Queen does not receive a salary for what she does; but she is - or ought to be - maintained in accordance with her high status (which goes to explain why it is pointless to tax her revenues, which are spent on conducting the monarchy).

The Oath-taking at the Coronation is therefore of great significance in the government of the State. But it is also important to each of us, personally. We expect the Queen to carry out her solemn promise – and she does, nobly. She sets the pattern.

In that excellent play, *A Man for all Seasons*, at the end of his trial Sir Thomas More confronts the perjurer, Richard Rich, and asks him about the medal he is wearing. Cromwell says, abruptly: 'Sir Richard is appointed Attorney-General for Wales'. 'For Wales?' says Sir Thomas. 'Why, Richard, it profits a man nothing to give his soul for the whole world... But for Wales!'

The Archbishop shall minister these questions; and the Queen, having a book in her hands, shall answer each question severally as follows:

Archbishop: 'Will you solemnly promise and swear to govern the Peoples of the United Kingdom of Great Britain and Northern Ireland, Canada, Australia, New Zealand, the Union of South Africa, Pakistan and Ceylon, and of your Possessions and the other Territories to any of them belonging or pertaining, according to their respective laws and customs?'

Queen: 'I solemnly promise so to do.'

In 1953 these represented the dominions and colonies of what was once the British Empire, now the Commonwealth of Nations. In a future coronation some of the names will have gone and it may be appropriate to insert here a general commitment to act as Head of the Commonwealth. But it is important to note that, because of this connection, the ceremony of coronation belongs to a world-wide, English-speaking people; and it cannot therefore be left to the monkeying of ministers in this country, should they wish to curtail or 'modernise' the event.

And yet, it is suggested, it is quite an event in human history, this dedication of one person to act as Head of a vast Commonwealth of some 1.4 billion people. Could this consecration account for the fact that, on the whole, the English-speaking peoples of the world understand and value freedom, decency and the rule of law? Do they find it established for them in the words of the ceremony? History shows that when persecution and horror descend like foul night on parts of the world, the inclination is always to turn to the light which still shines brightly in the English-speaking lands. Edmund Burke once said, of the American colonies:[1]

> As long as you [House of Commons] have the wisdom to keep the sovereign authority of this country as the sanctuary of liberty, the sacred temple consecrated to our common faith, wherever the chosen race and sons of England worship freedom, they will turn their faces towards you. The more they multiply, the more friends you will have; the more

1.   Speech on Conciliation with America

ardently they love liberty, the more perfect will be their obedience. Slavery they can have anywhere. It is a weed that grows in every soil. They may have it from Spain, they may have it from Prussia. But, until you become lost to all feeling of your true interest and your natural dignity, freedom they can have from none but you.

Freedom is thus a precious gift of the English-speaking peoples; but it is freedom under law.

Archbishop: 'Will you to your power cause Law and Justice, in Mercy, to be executed in all your judgments?'

Queen: 'I will.'

How can the Queen swear such an oath when she is not allowed to sit in judgment in the Courts? In the famous case of *Prohibitions del Roy*[1] Chief Justice Coke and his brother judges told King James firmly that he could not judge cases for himself:

> ...it is commonly said in our books that the King is always present in court in the judgment of law;... but the judgments are always given per curiam; and the Judges are sworn to execute justice according to law and custom of England... And the Judges informed the King, that no King after the conquest assumed to himself to give any judgment in any cause whatsoever, which concerned the administration of justice within this realm, but these were solely determined in the Courts of Justice...

This case also makes it clear that the monarch's presence is in each and every Court, as evidenced by the royal coat-of-arms; but the Queen can only swear such an oath in the clear understanding that the Judges who represent her will act according to their judicial oaths:

> I ... do swear that I will well and truly serve our Sovereign Lady Queen Elizabeth in the office of..., and I will do right to all manner of people after the laws and usages of this realm, without fear or favour, affection or ill will. So help me God.

In the light of this part of the coronation oath, it is therefore of

---

1. [1607] 12 Co. Rep. 63

the greatest importance that men and women selected to be judges should be persons of the utmost probity: never elected, but chosen, preferably by their fellow lawyers and judges, from long experience of the law, to 'cause Law and Justice, in Mercy, to be executed in all [their] judgments'.

Similarly, oath-taking runs throughout the scheme of government. The Oath of Allegiance, which every soldier takes, is as follows:

> I ... do swear that I will be faithful and bear true allegiance to Her Majesty Queen Elizabeth, her heirs and successors, according to law. So help me God.

The 'Form of Declaration' set out in a schedule to the Police Act 1996 is required from every new policeman or policewoman:

> I ... of ... do solemnly and sincerely declare and affirm that I will well and truly serve Our Sovereign Lady the Queen in the office of constable, without favour or affection, malice or ill will; and that I will to the best of my power cause the peace to be kept and preserved, and prevent all offences against the persons and properties of Her Majesty's subjects; and that while I continue to hold the said office I will to the best of my skill and knowledge discharge all the duties thereof faithfully according to law.

Not much doubt there as to the duties of a police officer. Compare it, however, with the proposed new Declaration for police officers to make, arising from the Patten Commission's recommendations: 'I hereby do solemnly and sincerely and truly declare and affirm that I will faithfully discharge the duties of the office of constable, and that in doing so I will act with fairness, integrity, diligence and impartiality, uphold fundamental human rights and accord equal respect to all individuals and to their traditions and beliefs'. Nothing about the Queen; nothing about keeping the peace; and, faced with trouble on the streets, which 'fundamental human right' should the officer apply to the situation in hand? It is a recipe for confusion and fear.

An oath, which binds anyone's honour, should be clear, precise, and free of doubt.

Why does the Archbishop say 'Law *and* Justice'? Law, ultimately, is the Will of God in creation: see Blackstone's *Commentaries on the Laws of England*. In course of time, there came to be an acceptance of the idea that law is the Will of the State: see Rousseau, for example. But the will of the state is a weak thing, easily brushed aside by events; whereas God's Law, Natural Law, is permanent and unchanging.

Justice is how the Law of God can be applied to any situation. What justice requires, says Plato, is the 'opinion of the best' as to what is best for the whole life of man, 'even if it be sometimes mistaken'. Injustice, on the other hand, is where the emotions take over, and things are decided in an atmosphere of anger and fear, pleasure and pain, jealousies and desires. Reason, says Plato, - 'the golden cord of reason' - is the common law of the state. Nothing should be decided judicially on the basis of emotions running counter to reason. [1]

'in Mercy' Mercy is a prerogative of the Crown: that is to say, it is 'beyond question' that the Crown should be able to exercise mercy. Justice and mercy run together: it is not just, for example, to treat everyone equally; it is merciful to treat each person according to that person's needs. If a man commits a crime, and shows every sign of penitence, then it may be possible to show him mercy and alleviate his punishment. This is because the law cannot be gainsaid: it will have its effect, somewhere, sometime. That being so, it is possible, with full knowledge, to excuse the sin and have the penalty paid by the community at large. The law is inescapable: someone must pay the penalty. This was the reason for the rise of the Lord Chancellor in this country, the 'keeper of the king's conscience', who traditionally was a cleric and capable

---

1.   *Laws*, 645 and 864

of understanding the spiritual significance of an act. He would advise the king as to exercising mercy if he 'with knowledge' (conscience) could say that the recipient would lead a good life thereafter, and the consequences of the guilty act could be borne by the country. A modern example is that of Richard Nixon, the first President of the United States to resign his high office because of complicity in crime: but he was pardoned by the incoming President, Gerald Ford, who personally had to pay the price of not being re-elected; and the United States as a whole had to bear the consequences of the crime at such a high level in its life. The consequences were that the situation would repeat, with other Presidents, such as Clinton, abusing office, until Americans realise the importance of electing what Jefferson called a 'natural aristocrat', that is to say, someone of integrity and honesty who would not mislead the people. Mercy with regard to Nixon was extended without any knowledge of its implications.

Archbishop: 'Will you to the utmost of your power maintain the Laws of God and the true profession of the Gospel? Will you to the utmost of your power maintain in the United Kingdom the Protestant Reformed Religion established by law? Will you maintain and preserve inviolably the settlement of the Church of England, and the doctrine, worship, discipline, and government thereof, as by law established in England? And will you preserve unto the Bishops and Clergy of England, and to the Churches there committed to their charge, all such rights and privileges, as by law do or shall appertain to them or any of them?'

Queen: 'All this I promise to do.'

This part of the oath is likely to prove contentious at the next coronation. Why should the 'Protestant Reformed Religion' be singled out for protection, when there are dozens of religious establishments in the country, each entitled to respect as a 'Human Right'? Particularly it will offend those who see 'Protestant Reformed Religion' as the cause of bitterness in Ireland.

There seems to be little doubt, however, that Protestant Christianity seems to suit the independence of the English. They are not
likely, generally, to embrace the spiritual control of the Pope, however much they respect him. Someone once observed, shrewdly,
that Canterbury Cathedral was a monument not to Becket, but to
the Black Prince. The English like to have their own national
church. It is part of the fabric of the State, as Anson observed. We
consider that, having 26 bishops sitting in the House of Lords, the
spiritual guidance they can offer to government must be beneficial.
It seems a faint hope, sometimes, when one considers the divisive
legislation produced on the questions of abortion and divorce.
However, let us just consider one contribution, of a very fine order,
from the Bishop of London in the debate in the House of Lords on
the war against Yugoslavia over Kosovo (6th May 1999):[1]

> Rather than recapitulating on matters in which other noble Lords are far
> more expert, perhaps I may speak as the Bishop responsible for rela-
> tions with the Orthodox churches.
>
> The noble Lord, Lord Merlyn-Rees, spoke about his personal experi-
> ence of the spirit in Yugoslavia. There is another side to the story. There
> is a democratic opposition in Yugoslavia, and there are people who are
> very clear about the nature of the challenge facing those societies. It is
> good to note that just before this action took place, religious leaders of
> the three main faith communities in Kosovo, the Moslems, the 60,000
> or so Roman Catholics and the Orthodox Church, were trying to pro-
> mote grass-root dialogue. Centres such as the Decani monastery have
> been havens and centres of relief for victims of the fighting, irrespective
> of ethnicity or religion...
>
> The expansion of NATO to embrace former Warsaw Pact countries,
> effected with so little turbulence, was a huge achievement. But it was an
> achievement built on the doctrine that NATO was a purely defensive
> alliance. We may not see matters in this way, but Russia has centuries
> of experience of invasion, not least from the West, and has a sense of
> vulnerability and a corresponding determination to ensure her own

1.   *Hansard*, cols. 815-817

security which it would be unwise to under-estimate. There is unanimity right across the Russian political spectrum that the NATO attack on Serbia introduces a dangerous unpredictability into relations within Europe. Many Russians are asking, 'Are we next?' ... Again, the potential role of the hugely numerous and significant Russian Orthodox Church in this peace-building effort should not be under-estimated...

In this context there is a clear need to look urgently at reform of the United Nations. If it is true that the Security Council is paralysed by its present structure, then surely there must be pressure for change, led by the governments of the democratic world. Cynicism about the UN is a luxury that we cannot afford. A global trading system and global communications call out for global institutions, which can be powerful advocates and protectors of the human rights and obligations of all world citizens...

The Bishop of London speaks with a very English common sense, clothed with the dignity of the national church. It is how we like our national church to be. Whatever adjustments are made, to accommodate other faiths into the Coronation Service, the Church of England should still take prime place. Edmund Burke spoke truly when he said:[1] 'We know, and, what is better, we feel inwardly, that religion is the basis of civil society, and the source of all good, and of all comfort'.

The Presenting of the Holy Bible

Archbishop: 'Our gracious Queen: to keep your Majesty ever mindful of the Law and the Gospel of God as the Rule for the whole life and government of Christian Princes, we present you with this Book, the most valuable thing that this world affords.'

And the Moderator [of the Church of Scotland] shall continue: 'Here is Wisdom; This is the royal Law; These are the lively Oracles of God'.

'the Rule for the whole life and government' These words

1. *Reflections*, [1790].

are important. There can be no doubt that the scriptures inform and guide us as to the 'whole life', not just the burdens of everyday living (in politics as elsewhere). Lord Denning put it this way: [1]

> ...if we seek truth and justice, we cannot find it by argument and debate, nor by reading and thinking, but only by the maintenance of true religion and virtue. Religion concerns the spirit in man whereby he is able to recognise what is truth and what is justice; whereas law is only the application, however imperfectly, of truth and justice in our everyday affairs. If religion perishes in the land, truth and justice will also. We have already strayed too far from the faith of our fathers. Let us return to it, for it is the only thing that can save us.

'Here is Wisdom; This is the royal Law; These are the lively Oracles of God' King Alfred the Great prefaced his collection of laws with some 40 verses, extracted from the Book of Exodus in the Bible. At the end he says: [2]

> These are the dooms which the Almighty God himself spake unto Moses, and commanded him to keep: and after the only begotten son of the Lord, our God, that is, our Saviour Christ, came on earth, he said that he came not to break nor to forbid these commandments, but with all good to increase them: and mercy and humility he taught. Then, after his Passion, before his Apostles were dispersed throughout all the earth, teaching, and while they were yet together, many heathen nations they turned to God. When they were all assembled, they sent messengers to Antioch and to Syria, to teach the law of Christ. But when they understood that it speeded them not, then sent they a letter unto them. Now this is the letter which all the Apostles sent to Antioch, and to Syria, and to Cilicia, which now from heathen nations are turned to Christ: 'The Apostles and the elder brethren wish you health: and we make known unto you, that we have heard that some of our fellows have come to you with our words, and have commanded you to observe a heavier rule than we commanded them, and have too much misled you with manifold commands, and have subverted more of your souls than they have directed... It seemed to the Holy Ghost and to us, that we should set no

---

1. *The Changing Law* [Stevens 1953], p. 122
2. *Ancient Laws*, op. cit., p. 25 *et seq.*

burthen upon you above that which it was needful for you to bear: now that is, that ye forbear from worshipping idols... and that which ye will that other men do not unto you, do ye not that to other men.

From this one doom a man may remember that he judge every one right-eously; he need no other doom-book. Let him remember that he adjudge to no man that which he would not that he should adjudge to him, if he sought judgment against him.

It is a long time since we prefaced our laws with this kind of testament. But at least prayers are said before the commencement of the day's business in the Lords and Commons. These empha-sise how important it is to *start* from a spiritual centre, a sense of one-ness, no matter what the business is that follows.

The Anointing

This holy part of the Ceremony is concerned with the consecration (making sacred) of the Queen. How many constitutions in the world today consecrate their Head of State? For the most part these Heads of State swear to uphold a written constitution; but what power enables them to do that? How can they enforce a con-stitution which is under threat? A consecrated Queen, however, carries with her a religious force which it is difficult to deny. When Charles I was executed a great guilt descended on the nation; and a great relief and joy at the return of Charles II. In Paris, even today, there is a sadness and a sense of loss at what they did to Louis XVI and Marie Antoinette (see, for example, the chapel dedicated to her in the Conciergerie). This is why having a Queen was important to the Australians when they turned to her following the dismissal of Gough Whitlam as Prime Minister: they wanted to know whether she would support the action of the Governor-General. The monarch does not need formal *powers:* she already has what she needs by way of *influence.*

Edmund Burke wrote:[1]

---

1. *Reflections* [1790]

This consecration is made, that all who administer in the government of men, in which they stand in the person of God Himself, should have high and worthy notions of their function and destination; that their hope should be full of immortality; that they should not look to the paltry pelf of the moment, nor to the temporary and transient praise of the vulgar, but to a solid, permanent existence, in the permanent part of their nature, and to a permanent fame and glory, in the example they leave as a rich inheritance to the world.

Archbishop: 'O Lord and heavenly Father, the exalter of the humble and the strength of thy chosen, who by anointing with Oil didst of old make and consecrate kings, priests and prophets, to teach and govern thy people Israel: Bless and sanctify thy chosen servant ELIZABETH, who by our office and ministry is now to be anointed with this Oil, and consecrated Queen: Strengthen her, O Lord, with the Holy Ghost the Comforter; Confirm and stablish her with thy free and princely Spirit, the Spirit of wisdom and government, the Spirit of counsel and ghostly strength, the Spirit of knowledge and true godliness, and fill her, O Lord, with the Spirit of thy holy fear, now and for ever; through Jesus Christ our Lord. Amen.'

The Investiture

Then shall the Archbishop take the Sword of State from off the altar, and... shall deliver it into the Queen's hands; and, the Queen holding it, the Archbishop shall say: 'Receive this kingly Sword, brought now from the altar of God, and delivered to you by the hands of us the Bishops and servants of God, though unworthy. With this Sword do justice, stop the growth of iniquity, protect the Holy Church of God, help and defend widows and orphans, restore the things that are gone to decay, maintain the things that are restored, punish and reform what is amiss, and confirm what is in good order: that doing these things you may be glorious in all virtue; and so faithfully serve our Lord Jesus Christ in this life, that you may reign for ever with Him in the life which is to come. Amen.'

'The Sword of State' is a reminder of the ancient orders of mankind, spoken about in scriptures, in which the first is the priestly, caring for the soul; secondly, the warrior and ruling class, symbolised by this Sword; thirdly, the merchants who create wealth; and fourthly, those who labour. The monarch has care of all these, as is indicated in the above passage. That care is exercised through watchfulness: that is what is required of the Queen, that she be eternally vigilant. A Prime Minister does well to recognise that he answers to the Queen for conduct of affairs. The sword is contained in the questions she puts to him. Bagehot is a shrewd commentator:[1]

> To state the matter shortly, the sovereign has, under a constitutional monarchy such as ours, three rights – the right to be consulted, the right to encourage, the right to warn. And a king of great sense and sagacity would want no others. He would find that his having no others would enable him to use these with singular effect. He would say to his minister: 'The responsibility of these measures is upon you. Whatever you think best must be done. Whatever you think best shall have my full and effectual support. But you will observe that for this reason and that reason what you propose to do is bad; for this reason and that reason what you do not propose is better. I do not oppose, it is my duty not to oppose; but observe that I warn'. Supposing the king to be right, and to have what kings often have, the gift of effectual expression, he could not help moving his minister. He might not always turn his course, but he would always trouble his mind.

The astonishing care shown by King Alfred for all classes of men is reflected in the following passage:[2]

> You know that covetousness and greed for worldly dominion never pleased me over much, and that I did not all too greatly desire this earthly rule, but yet I desired tools and material for the work that I was charged to perform, namely that I might worthily and fittingly steer and rule the dominion that was entrusted to me. You know that no man can

1.   *Works*, Vol. V, p. 253
2.   *English Historical Documents*, Vol. I, pp 845-6

reveal any talent or rule and steer any dominion without tools and material. That without which one cannot carry on that craft is the material of
every craft. This, then, is a king's material and his tools for ruling with,
that he have his land fully manned. He must have men who pray and soldiers and workmen. Lo, you know that without these tools no king can
reveal his skill. Also, this is his material, which he must have for these
tools – sustenance for those three orders; and their sustenance consists
of land to live on, and gifts, and weapons, and food, and ale, and clothes,
and whatever else those three orders require. And without these things
he cannot hold those tools, nor without those tools do any of the things
that he is charged to do. For that reason I desired material to rule that
dominion with, that my powers and dominion would not be forgotten
and concealed. For every talent and every dominion is soon worn out
and silently passed over, if it is without wisdom; because no man can
bring forth any craft without wisdom, for whatever is done in folly can
never be accounted as a craft. In brief, I desired to live worthily as long
as I lived, and to leave after my life, to the men who should come after,
my memory in good works.

*The Archbishop presents the symbols of majesty to the Queen.
Among them are:* 'Receive this Imperial Robe, and the Lord your
God endue you with knowledge and wisdom, with majesty and
with power from on high; the Lord clothe you with the robe of
righteousness, and with the garments of salvation. Amen.'

'Receive this Orb set under the Cross, and remember that the
whole world is subject to the Power and Empire of Christ our
Redeemed.'

'Receive the Royal Sceptre, the ensign of kingly power and
justice.'

'Receive the Rod of equity and mercy. Be so merciful that you
be not too remiss, so execute justice that you forget not mercy.
Punish the wicked, protect and cherish the just, and lead your
people in the way wherein they should go.'

'Lead your people in the way wherein they should go'
reminds one of the chariot analogy, mentioned before, with the

Sovereign as the charioteer, the reins as Parliament, the people being the horses and their desires the roads down which they would go. The analogy suggests that a light touch of the reins is required to steer the people into safe paths of conduct.

But the passenger in the chariot of the body is the Self – everyone's true self. And these symbols are meant to remind us of self-respect: respect for ourselves as individuals, as families, for the nation and for the whole of mankind. Self-respect is sovereignty. Without self-respect there is no sovereignty. Thus, in these glittering circumstances, we are reminded of our own worth, as a people loving freedom. Emerson said: 'We are symbols, and inhabit symbols'.[1]

The paramount symbol in the Coronation Service is the Crown of St Edward:

The Archbishop: 'O God, the Crown of the faithful; Bless we beseech thee this Crown, and so sanctify thy servant ELIZABETH upon whose head thou dost place it for a sign of royal majesty, that she may be filled by thine abundant grace with all princely virtues: through the King eternal Jesus Christ our Lord. Amen.'

Then the Queen still sitting in King Edward's Chair, the Archbishop, assisted with other Bishops, shall come from the Altar; the Dean of Westminster shall bring the Crown, and the Archbishop taking it of him shall reverently put it upon the Queen's head. At the sight whereof the people, with loud and repeated shouts shall cry:

GOD SAVE THE QUEEN

The Princes and Princesses, the Peers and Peeresses shall put on their coronets and caps, and the Kings of Arms their crowns; and the trumpets shall sound, and by a signal given, the great guns at the Tower shall be shot off.

---

1.   *Essays*, The Poet

Appendix I

The Form and Order of
Queen Elizabeth II's Coronation

I. The Preparation

In the morning upon the day of the Coronation early, care is to be taken that the Ampulla be filled with the Oil for the anointing, and, together with the Spoon, be laid ready upon the Altar in the Abbey Church.

The Litany shall be sung as the Dean and Prebendaries and the choir of Westminster proceed from the Altar to the west door of the Church.

The Archbishops being already vested in their Copes and Mitres and the Bishops Assistant in their Copes, the procession shall be formed immediately outside of the west door of the Church, and shall wait till notice be given of the approach of her Majesty, and shall then begin to move into the Church.

And the people shall remain standing from the Entrance until the beginning of the Communion Service.

II. The Entrance to the Church

The Queen, as soon as she enters at the west door of the Church, is to be received with this Anthem:

Psalm cxxii. i-3, 6, 7.

I WAS glad when they said unto me, We will go into the house of the Lord. Our feet shall stand in thy gates, O Jerusalem. Jerusalem is built as a city that is at unity in itself. O pray for the peace of Jerusalem: they shall prosper that love thee. Peace be within thy walls, and plenteousness within thy palaces.

The Queen shall in the mean time pass up through the body of the Church, into and through the choir, and so up the stairs to the Theatre; and having passed by her Throne, she shall make her humble adoration, and then kneeling at the faldstool set for her before her Chair of Estate on the south side of the Altar, use some short private prayers; and after, sit down in her Chair.

The Bible, Paten, and Chalice shall meanwhile be brought by the Bishops who had borne them, and placed upon the Altar.

Then the Lords who carry in procession the Regalia, except those who carry the Swords, shall come from their places and present in order every one what he carries to the Archbishop, who shall deliver them to the Dean of Westminster, to be by him placed upon the Altar.

III. The Recognition

The Archbishop, together with the Lord Chancellor, Lord Great Chamberlain, Lord High Constable, and Earl Marshal (Garter King of Arms preceding them), shall then go to the East side of the Theatre, and after shall go to the other three sides in this order, South, West, and North, and at every of the four sides the Archbishop shall with a loud voice speak to the People: and the Queen in the meanwhile, standing up by King Edward's Chair, shall turn and show herself unto the People at every of the four sides of the Theatre as the Archbishop is at every of them, the Archbishop saying:

SIRS, I here present unto you Queen ELIZABETH, your undoubted Queen:

Wherefore all you who are come this day to do your homage and service, Are you willing to do the same?

The People signify their willingness and joy, by loud and repeated acclamations, all with one voice crying out,

GOD SAVE QUEEN ELIZABETH.

Then the trumpets shall sound.

IV. The Oath

The Queen having returned to her Chair, (her Majesty having already on Tuesday, the 4th day of November, 1952 in the presence of the two Houses of Parliament, made and signed the Declaration prescribed by Act of Parliament), the Archbishop standing before her shall administer the Coronation Oath, first asking the Queen,

Madam, is your Majesty willing to take the Oath?

And the Queen answering,

I am willing.

The Archbishop shall minister these questions; and the Queen, having a book in her hands, shall answer each question severally as follows:

Archbishop: Will you solemnly promise and swear to govern the Peoples of the United Kingdom of Great Britain and Northern Ireland, Canada, Australia, New Zealand, the Union of South Africa, Pakistan, and Ceylon, and of your Possessions and the other Territories to any of them belonging or pertaining, according to their respective laws and customs?

Queen: I solemnly promise so to do.

Archbishop: Will you to your power cause Law and Justice, in Mercy, to be executed in all your judgements?

Queen: I will.

Archbishop: Will you to the utmost of your power maintain the Laws of God and the true profession of the Gospel? Will you to the utmost of your power maintain in the United Kingdom the Protestant Reformed Religion established by law? Will you maintain and preserve inviolably the settlement of the Church of England, and the doctrine, worship, discipline, and government thereof, as by law established in England? And will you preserve unto the Bishops and Clergy of England, and to the Churches there committed to their charge, all such rights and privileges, as by law do or shall appertain to them or any of them?

Queen: All this I promise to do.

Then the Queen arising out of her Chair, supported as before, the Sword of State being carried before her, shall go to the Altar, and make her solemn Oath in the sight of all the people to observe the premisses: laying her right hand upon the Holy Gospel in the great Bible (which was before carried in the procession and is now brought from the Altar by the Archbishop, and tendered to her as she kneels upon the steps), and saying these words:

The things which I have here before promised, I will perform and keep. So help me God.

Then the Queen shall kiss the Book and sign the Oath.

The Queen having thus taken her Oath shall return again to her Chair, and the Bible shall be delivered to the Dean of Westminster.

V. The Presenting of the Holy Bible

When the Queen is again seated, the Archbishop shall go to her Chair: and the Moderator of the General Assembly of the Church of Scotland, receiving the Holy Bible from the Dean of Westminster, shall bring it to the Queen and present it to her, the Archbishop saying these words:

OUR GRACIOUS QUEEN: to keep your Majesty ever mindful of the Law and the Gospel of God as the Rule for the whole life and government of Christian Princes, we present you with this Book, the most valuable thing that this world affords.

And the Moderator shall continue:

Here is Wisdom; This is the royal Law; These are the lively Oracles of God.

Then shall the Queen deliver back the Bible to the Moderator who shall bring it to the Dean of Westminster, to be reverently placed again upon the Altar. This done, the Archbishop shall return to the Altar.

VI. The Beginning of the Communion Service

THE INTROIT

Psalm lxxxiv. 9, 10

Behold, O God our defender: and look upon the face of thine Anointed. For one day in thy courts: is better than a thousand.

Then, the Queen with the people kneeling, the Archbishop shall begin the Communion Service saying:

ALMIGHTY GOD, unto whom all hearts be open, all desires known, and from whom no secrets are hid: Cleanse the thoughts of our hearts by the inspiration of thy Holy Spirit, that we may perfectly love thee, and worthily magnify thy holy Name; through Christ our Lord. Amen.

Archbishop: Lord have mercy upon us.

Answer: Christ have mercy upon us.

Archbishop: Lord have mercy upon us. Let us pray.

O GOD, who providest for thy people by thy power, and rulest over them in love:

Grant unto this thy servant ELIZABETH, our Queen, the Spirit of wisdom and government, that being devoted unto thee with her whole heart, she may so wisely govern, that in her time thy Church may be in safety, and Christian devotion may continue in peace; that so persevering in good works unto the end, she may by thy mercy come to thine everlasting kingdom; through Jesus Christ, thy Son, our Lord, who liveth and reigneth with thee in the unity of the Holy Ghost, one God for ever and ever.

Amen.

THE EPISTLE

To be read by one of the Bishops.

I St. Peter ii. 13

SUBMIT yourselves to every ordinance of man for the Lord's sake: whether it be to the king, as supreme; or unto governors, as unto them that are sent by him for the punishment of evildoers, and for the praise of them that do well. For so is the will of God, that with well doing ye may put to silence the ignorance of foolish men: as free, and not using your liberty for a cloke of maliciousness, but as the servants of God. Honour all men. Love the brotherhood. Fear God. Honour the king.

THE GRADUAL

Psalm cxli. 2

LET my prayer come up into thy presence as the incense: and let the lifting up of my hands be as an evening sacrifice.

Alleluia.

THE GOSPEL

To be read by another Bishop, the Queen with the people standing.

St Matthew xxii. 15

THEN went the Pharisees, and took counsel how they might entangle him in his talk. And they sent out unto him their disciples, with the Herodians, saying Master, we know that thou art true, and teachest the way of God in truth, neither carest thou for any man: for thou regardest not the person of men. Tell us therefore, What thinkest thou? Is it lawful to give tribute unto Caesar, or not? But Jesus perceived their wickedness, and said, Why tempt ye me, ye hypocrites? Shew me the tribute-money. And they brought unto him a penny. And he saith unto them, Whose is this image and superscription? They say unto him, Caesar's. Then saith he unto them, Render therefore unto Caesar the things which are Caesar's: and unto God the things that are God's. When they had heard these words they marvelled, and left him, and went their way.

And the Gospel ended, shall be sung the Creed following, the Queen with the people standing, as before.

I BELIEVE in one God the Father Almighty, Maker of heaven and earth, And of all things visible and invisible:

And in one Lord Jesus Christ, the only begotten Son of God, Begotten of his Father before all worlds, God of God, Light of Light, Very God of very God, Begotten, not made, Being of one substance with the Father, By whom all things were made:

Who for us men, and for our salvation came down from heaven, And was incarnate by the Holy Ghost of the Virgin Mary, And was made man, And was crucified also for us under Pontius Pilate. He suffered and was buried, And the third day he rose again according to the Scriptures, And ascended into heaven, And sitteth on the right hand of the Father. And he shall come again with glory to judge both the quick and the dead: Whose kingdom shall have no end.

And I believe in the Holy Ghost, The Lord and giver of life, Who proceedeth from the Father and the Son, Who with the Father and the Son together is worshipped and glorified, Who spake by the Prophets. And I believe one Catholick and Apostolick Church. I acknowledge one Baptism for the remission of sins. And I look for the Resurrection of the dead, And the life of the world to come. Amen.

VII. The Anointing

The creed being ended, the Queen kneeling at her faldstool, and the people kneeling in their places, the Archbishop shall begin the hymn, VENI, CREATOR SPIRITUS, and the choir shall sing it out.

Come, Holy Ghost, our souls inspire,
And lighten with celestial fire.
Thou the anointing Spirit art,
Who dost thy seven-fold gifts impart.

Thy blessed Unction from above
Is comfort, life, and fire of love.
Enable with perpetual light
The dulness of our blinded sight.

Anoint and cheer our soiled face
With the abundance of thy grace:
Keep far our foes, give peace at home;
Where thou art guide, no ill can come.

Teach us to know the Father, Son,
And thee, of both, to be but One;
That, through the ages all along,
This may be our endless song:

Praise to thy eternal merit,
Father, Son, and Holy Spirit.

The hymn being ended the Archbishop shall say:

Let us pray:

O LORD and heavenly Father, the exalter of the humble and the strength of thy chosen, who by anointing with Oil didst of old make and consecrate kings, priests, and prophets, to teach and govern thy people Israel: Bless and sanctify thy chosen servant ELIZABETH, who by our office and ministry is now to be anointed with this Oil, and consecrated Queen: Strengthen her, O Lord, with the Holy

Ghost the Comforter; Confirm and stablish her with thy free and princely Spirit, the Spirit of wisdom and government, the Spirit of counsel and ghostly strength, the Spirit of knowledge and true godliness, and fill her, O Lord, with the Spirit of thy holy fear, now and for ever; through Jesus Christ our Lord.

Amen.

This prayer being ended, and the people standing, the choir shall sing:

I Kings i. 39, 40

ZADOK the priest and Nathan the prophet anointed Solomon king; and all the people rejoiced and said: God save the king, Long live the king, May the king live for ever. Amen. Hallelujah.

In the mean time, the Queen rising from her devotions, having been disrobed of her crimson robe by the Lord Great Chamberlain, assisted by the Mistress of the Robes, and being uncovered, shall go before the Altar, supported and attended as before.

The Queen shall sit down in King Edward's Chair (placed in the midst of the Area over against the Altar, with a faldstool before it), wherein she is to be anointed. Four Knights of the Garter shall hold over her a rich pall of silk, or cloth of gold: the Dean of Westminster, taking the Ampulla and Spoon from off the Altar, shall hold them ready, pouring some of the holy Oil into the Spoon, and with it the Archbishop shall anoint the Queen in the form of a cross:

On the palms of both the hands, saying, Be thy Hands anointed with holy Oil.

On the breast, saying,

Be thy Breast anointed with holy Oil.

On the crown of the head, saying,

Be thy Head anointed with holy Oil: as kings, priests, and prophets were anointed:

And as Solomon was anointed king by Zadok the priest and Nathan the prophet, so be thou anointed, blessed, and consecrated Queen over the Peoples, whom the Lord thy God hath given thee to rule and govern, In the Name of the Father, and of the Son, and of the Holy Ghost. Amen.

Then shall the Dean of Westminster lay the Ampulla and Spoon upon the Altar; and the Queen kneeling down at the fald-stool, the Archbishop shall say this Blessing over her:

OUR Lord Jesus Christ, the Son of God, who by his Father was anointed with the Oil of gladness above his fellows, by his holy Anointing pour down upon your Head and Heart the blessing of the Holy Ghost, and prosper the works of your Hands: that by the assistance of his heavenly grace you may govern and preserve the Peoples committed to your charge in wealth, peace, and godliness; and after a long and glorious course of ruling a temporal kingdom wisely, justly, and religiously, you may at last be made partaker of an eternal kingdom, through the same Jesus Christ our Lord. Amen.

This prayer being ended, the Queen shall arise and sit down again in King Edward's Chair, while the Knights of the Garter bear away the pall; whereupon the Queen again arising, the Dean of Westminster, assisted by the Mistress of the Robes, shall put upon her Majesty the Colobium Sindonis and the Supertunica or Close Pall of cloth of gold, together with a Girdle of the same. Then shall the Queen again sit down; and after her, the people also.

VIII. The Presenting of the Spurs and Sword, and the Oblation of the said Sword

The Spurs shall be brought from the Altar by the Dean of West-minster, and delivered to the Lord Great Chamberlain; who, kneeling down, shall present them to the Queen, who forthwith sends them back to the Altar.

Then the Lord who carries the Sword of State, delivering to the Lord Chamberlain the said Sword (which is thereupon deposited in Saint Edward's Chapel) shall receive from the Lord Chamberlain, in lieu thereof, another Sword in a scabbard which he shall deliver to the Archbishop: and the Archbishop shall lay it on the Altar and say:

HEAR our prayers, O Lord, we beseech thee, and so direct and support thy servant Queen ELIZABETH, that she may not bear the Sword in vain; but may use it as the minister of God for the terror and punishment of evildoers, and for the protection and encouragement of those that do well, through Jesus Christ our Lord.

Amen.

Then shall the Archbishop take the Sword from off the Altar, and (the Archbishop of York and the Bishops of London and Winchester and other Bishops assisting and going along with him) shall deliver it into the Queen's hands; and, the Queen holding it, the Archbishop shall say:

RECEIVE this kingly Sword, brought now from the Altar of God, and delivered to you by the hands of us the Bishops and servants of God, though unworthy. With this Sword do justice, stop the growth of iniquity, protect the holy Church of God, help and defend widows and orphans, restore the things that are gone to decay, maintain the things that are restored, punish and reform what is amiss, and confirm what is in good order: that doing these things you may be glorious in all virtue; and so faithfully serve our Lord Jesus Christ in this life, that you may reign for ever with him in the life which is to come.

Amen.

Then the Queen, rising up and going to the Altar shall offer it there in the scabbard, and then return and sit down in King

Edward's Chair: and the Peer, who first received the Sword, shall offer the price of it, namely, one hundred shillings, and having thus redeemed it, shall receive it from the Dean of Westminster, from off the Altar, and draw it out of the scabbard, and carry it naked before her Majesty during the rest of the solemnity.

Then the Archbishop of York and the Bishops who have assisted during the offering shall return to their places.

IX. The Investing with the Armills, the Stole Royal and the Robe Royal: and the Delivery of the Orb

Then the Dean of Westminster shall deliver the Armills to the Archbishop, who, putting them upon the Queen's wrists, shall say:

RECEIVE the Bracelets of sincerity and wisdom, both for tokens of the Lord's protection embracing you on every side; and also for symbols and pledges of that bond which unites you with your Peoples: to the end that you may be strengthened in all your works and defended against your enemies both bodily and ghostly, through Jesus Christ our Lord. Amen.

Then the Queen arising, the Robe Royal or Pall of cloth of gold with the Stole Royal shall be delivered by the Groom of the Robes to the Dean of Westminster, and by him, assisted by the Mistress of the Robes, put upon the Queen, standing; the Lord Great Chamberlain fastening the clasps. Then shall the Queen sit down, and the Archbishop shall say:

RECEIVE this Imperial Robe, and the Lord your God endue you with knowledge and wisdom, with majesty and with power from on high: the Lord clothe you with the robe of righteousness, and with the garments of salvation. Amen.

THE DELIVERY OF THE ORB

Then shall the Orb with the Cross be brought from the Altar by the Dean of Westminster and delivered into the Queen's right hand by the Archbishop, saying:

RECEIVE this Orb set under the Cross, and remember that the whole world is subject to the Power and Empire of Christ our Redeemer.

Then shall the Queen deliver the Orb to the Dean of Westminster, to be by him laid on the Altar.

X. The Investiture per Annulum, et per Sceptrum et Baculum

Then the Keeper of the Jewel House shall deliver to the Archbishop the Queen's Ring, wherein is set a sapphire and upon it a ruby cross: the Archbishop shall put it on the fourth finger of her Majesty' s right hand, and say:

RECEIVE the Ring of kingly dignity, and the seal of Catholic Faith: and as you are this day consecrated to be our Head and Prince, so may you continue stedfastly as the Defender of Christ's Religion; that being rich in faith and blessed in all good works, you may reign with him who is the Kings of Kings, to whom be the Glory for ever and ever. Amen.

Then shall the Dean of Westminster bring the Sceptre with the Cross and the Rod with the Dove to the Archbishop.

The Glove having been presented to the Queen, the Archbishop shall deliver the Sceptre with the Cross into the Queen's right hand, saying:

RECEIVE the Royal Sceptre, the ensign of kingly power and justice.

And then shall he deliver the Rod with the Dove into the Queen's left hand, and say:

RECEIVE the Rod of equity and mercy. Be so merciful that you be not too remiss; so execute justice that you forget not mercy. Punish the wicked, protect and cherish the just, and lead your people in the way wherein they should go.

XI. The Putting on of The Crown

Then the people shall rise; and the Archbishop, standing before the Altar, shall take the Crown into his hands, and laying it again before him upon the Altar, he shall say:

O GOD the Crown of the faithful: Bless we beseech thee this Crown, and so sanctify thy servant ELIZABETH upon whose head this day thou dost place it for a sign of royal majesty, that she may be filled by thine abundant grace with all princely virtues: through the King eternal Jesus Christ our Lord.

Amen.

Then the Queen still sitting in King Edward's Chair, the Archbishop, assisted with other Bishops, shall come from the Altar: the Dean of Westminster shall bring the Crown, and the Archbishop taking it of him shall reverently put it upon the Queen's head. At the sight whereof the people, with loud and repeated shouts, shall cry:

GOD SAVE THE QUEEN.

The Princes and Princesses, the Peers and Peeresses shall put on their coronets and caps, and the Kings of Arms their crowns; and the trumpets shall sound, and by a signal given, the great guns at the Tower shall be shot off.

The acclamation ceasing, the Archbishop shall go on, and say:

GOD crown you with a crown of glory and righteousness, that having a right faith and manifold fruit of good works, you may obtain the crown of an everlasting kingdom by the gift of him whose kingdom endureth for ever. Amen.

Then shall the choir sing:

Be strong and of a good courage: keep the commandments of the Lord thy God and walk in his ways.

And the people shall remain standing until after the Homage be ended.

XII. The Benediction

And now the Queen having been thus anointed and crowned, and having received all the ensigns of Royalty, the Archbishop shall solemnly bless her: and the Archbishop of York and all the Bishops, with the rest of the Peers and all the people, shall follow every part of the Benediction with a loud and hearty Amen.

THE Lord bless you and keep you. The Lord protect you in all your ways and prosper all your handywork. Amen.

The Lord give you faithful Parliaments and quiet Realms; sure defence against all enemies; fruitful lands and a prosperous industry; wise counsellors and upright magistrates; leaders of integrity in learning and labour; a devout, learned, and useful clergy; honest, peaceable, and dutiful citizens. Amen.

May Wisdom and Knowledge be the Stability of your Times, and the Fear of the Lord your Treasure. Amen.

The Lord who hath made you Queen over these Peoples give you increase of grace, honour, and happiness in this world, and make you partaker of his eternal felicity in the world to come.

Amen.

Then shall the Archbishop turn to the people and say:

AND the same Lord God Almighty grant, that the Clergy and Nobles assembled here for this great and solemn service, and together with them all the Peoples of this Commonwealth, fearing God, and honouring the Queen, may by the gracious assistance of God's infinite goodness, and by the vigilant care of his anointed servant, our gracious Sovereign, continually enjoy peace, plenty, and prosperity; through Jesus Christ our Lord, to whom, with the eternal Father, and God the Holy Ghost, be glory in the Church, world without end.

Amen.

XIII. The Enthroning

Then shall the Queen go to her Throne, and be lifted up into it by the Archbishops and Bishops, and other Peers of the Kingdom; and being enthroned, or placed therein, all the Great Officers, those that bear the Swords and the Sceptres, and the Nobles who carried the other Regalia, shall stand round about the steps of the Throne; and the Archbishop standing before the Queen, shall say:

STAND firm, and hold fast from henceforth the seat and state of royal and imperial dignity, which is this day delivered unto you, in the Name and by the Authority of Almighty God, and by the hands of us the Bishops and servants of God, though unworthy. And the Lord God Almighty, whose ministers we are, and the stewards of his mysteries, establish your Throne in righteousness, that it may stand fast for evermore. Amen.

Then follow:

The Homage

The Communion

The *Te Deum Laudamus*

and

The Recess

which are omitted from this appendix

****

Appendix II

Institutes of Polity, Civil and Ecclesiastical[1]

I. Of the Heavenly King

In the name of the Lord. There is one eternal King, Ruler and Maker of all creatures. He is rightfully King, and Glory of Kings, and of all kings best, who ever were, or shall be. To him be ever praise and glory, and eternal majesty, for evermore. Amen.

II. Of an Earthly King

It is the duty of a Christian king, in a Christian nation, to be, as it is right, the people's comfort, and a righteous shepherd over a Christian flock. And it is his duty, with all his power, to upraise Christianity, and everywhere further, and protect God's church; and establish peace among, and reconcile all Christian people, with just law, as he most diligently may, and in everything love righteousness, before God and before the world; because he shall thereby chiefly prosper himself, and his subjects also, because he loves justice, before God and before the world. And it is his duty earnestly to support those who desire right, and ever severely to punish those who desire perverseness. He shall evil-doing men vigorously chastise with secular punishment, and he shall robbers,

---

1. from the translation of the Anglo-Saxon text, printed in Thorpe, *Ancient Laws and Institutes of England*, [1840], attributed to Wulfstan, Archbishop of York, who died in 1023

and plunderers, and public spoilers, hate and suppress, and all God's foes sternly withstand; and rightly he shall be both mild and severe, mild to the good, and stern to the evil. That is a king's prerogative, and a kingly practice, and that in a nation shall be most effective. Lo! through what shall peace and support come to God's servants and to God's poor, save through Christ, and through a Christian king? Through the king's wisdom, the people become happy, well-conditioned, and victorious, and therefore shall a wise king magnify and honour Christianity and kingship, and he shall ever hinder and abhor heathenism. He shall very diligently listen to book-precepts, and zealously hold God's commandments, and frequently meditate wisdom with the *witan*[1], if he will rightly obey God. And if anyone be so violent, anywhere in the nation, that he will observe no law, so as he ought, but corrupts God's law, or obstructs the people's law, then be it announced to the king, if it be needful, and let him then forthwith decree respecting the *bot*[2], and strenuously compel him to that which is his duty, even forcibly, if he otherwise cannot; and let him do as it behoves him, let him purify his people before God, and before the world, if he will merit God's mercy.

III. Of a Kingdom

Eight are the columns which firmly bear up a lawful kingdom: truth, magnanimity, liberality, stedfastness, formidableness, promotion [of the good], lightness [of taxation], righteousness [of judgment]; and seven things are befitting a righteous king: first, that he have very great awe of God, and secondly, that he ever love righteousness, and thirdly, that he be humble before God, and

---

1. the supreme council of the nation, summoned by the king; and its members, besides the archbishop or archbishops, were the bishops, ealdormen, duces, eorls, thanes, abbots, priests and even deacons. In this assembly, laws, both secular and ecclesiastical, were promulgated and repealed, and charters of grants made by the king confirmed and ratified.
2. amends, atonement, compensation, indemnification.

fourthly, that he be rigid towards evil, and fifthly, that he comfort and feed God's poor, and sixthly, that he further and protect God's church, and seventhly, that, towards friends and towards strangers, he be guided alike to just judgment.

IV. Of a Throne

Every lawful throne, which stands perfectly erect, stands on three pillars: one is *oratores*, and the second is *laboratores*, and the third is *bellatores*. Oratores are supplicants, whose duty is to serve God, and earnestly intercede, both day and night, for the nation. Laboratores are workmen, who are to provide that by which all the people shall live. Bellatores are warriors, who are to defend the country martially with weapons. On these three pillars ought every throne rightfully to stand, in a Christian nation; and if either of them become weak, forthwith the throne will totter; and if either of them break, then will the throne fall down, and that is altogether to the nation's detriment; but let them be diligently fixed, and strengthened, and confirmed with the wise law of God, and just secular law, that will be to the lasting advantage of the nation: and true it is what I say, if Christianity be weakened, the kingdom will forthwith totter; and if bad laws be set up anywhere in the nation, or vicious habits be anywhere too much loved, that will be all to the nation's detriment: but let be done as it is requisite, let unrighteousness be suppressed, and God's righteousness upraised; that may be beneficial before God, and before the world. Amen.

V. Of the Chief 'Witan'

Kings and bishops, *eorls*[1] and *heretogs*[2], *reeves*[3] and judges, doctors and lawyers it rightly befits, before God and before the

---

1. Old Saxon 'erl', Old Norse 'jarl', signifies 'man', though generally applied to one of consideration, on account of his rank or valour.
2. 'leader of an army'
3. the 'shire-reeve' is familiar to us as the 'sheriff'. He was the fiscal officer of the shire, under the ealdorman or comes.

world, that they be of one mind, and love God's righteousness. And bishops are heralds, and teachers of God's law, and their duty is to preach [righteousness], and forbid unrighteousness, and he who disdains to listen to them, let that be in common with him and God himself. And if bishops neglect to correct sins and forbid unrighteousness, and make not known God's righteousness, but murmur with their throats, where they ought to cry out, woe to them for that silence! Of them spake the prophet, and thus angrily said: 'If thou', said our Lord, 'wilt not correct the sins of the sinful, and forbid unrighteousness, and make known to the wicked his wicked deeds, thou shalt bitterly pay for that soul'. This may be a heart-care to every bishop; let him bethink himself earnestly, according as he will. And he who will not properly hear God's preachers, nor attend to divine doctrine as he should; he shall hear foes, if he will not friends; because he is a contemner of God, who contemns God's preachers; as Christ himself in his gospel manifestly said, when he thus spake: 'Who heareth you, heareth me; and he who despiseth you, despiseth me'. Alas, heavy is the burden, which God's herald must bear, if he will not strenuously forbid unrighteousness; because though he himself do good, and another man does amiss, that shall injure him, if he will not correct [him]; and though God's herald do amiss, let not a man look to that, but mind his doctrine, if he teach what is good, so as Christ taught that a man should do, when he, in his Gospel, manifestly thus spake: 'Follow their doctrines, but not their sins'. No man ought ever, on account of the bishop's sins, to disregard himself, but let him follow his doctrines, if he teach well. And lo! beloved men, do as I enjoin, without anger; listen to what I say. I know very well myself to be wicked in word and deed all too much; nevertheless I dare not, through fear of God, be altogether silent regarding many of those things which injure this people.

VI. Of Bishops

Bishops shall follow their books and prayers, and daily and nightly, oft and frequently call to Christ, and earnestly intercede for all Christian people; and they shall learn, and rightly teach, and diligently inquire regarding the people's deeds; and they shall preach and earnestly give example, for the spiritual need of a Christian nation; and they shall not willingly consent to any unrighteousness, but earnestly support all righteousness; they shall have the fear of God in mind, and not be too slothful, for fear of the world; but let them ever earnestly preach God's righteousness and forbid unrighteousness; observe it who will: because weak will the shepherd be found for the flock, who will not defend, at least with his cry, the flock which he has to tend, unless he otherwise may, if any public robber there begin to rob. There is none so evil a robber as is the devil himself; he is always [busied] about that one thing -- how he may rob most among men's souls: therefore should the shepherds be very watchful, and diligently calling, who have to shield the people against this public robber. These are bishops and mass-priests, who have to protect and secure the godly flock with wise instructions, that the ferocious were-wolf do not too widely devastate, nor bite too many of the spiritual flock: and he who scorns to listen to them, be that between him and God himself. Alas! many are there, nevertheless, of those who heed but little, and care little for precepts of books, or instructions of bishops, and also hold lightly of blessings or curses, and understand not, as they ought, what Christ in his Gospel manifestly said, when he thus spake: *'Quis vos audit'* etc... Such is to be borne in mind, and God's anger ever to be guarded against. Now we also earnestly enjoin every man to follow God's precepts, and his laws; then will he earn for himself eternal joy.

VII. Likewise

To a bishop belongs every direction, both in divine and worldly things. He shall, in the first place, inform men in orders, so that each of them may know what properly it behoves him to do, and also what they have to enjoin to secular men. He shall ever be [busied] about reconciliation and peace, as he best may. He shall zealously appease strifes and effect peace, with those temporal judges who love right. He shall in accusations direct the *lad*[1], so that no man may wrong another, either in oath or in ordeal. He shall not consent to any injustice, or wrong measure, or false weight: but it is fitting that every legal right, (both *burh-riht*[2] and *land-riht*) go by his counsel, and with his witness; and let every burg-measure, and every balance for weighing, be, by his direction and furthering, very exact; lest any man should wrong another, and thereby altogether too greatly sin. He shall always shield Christian men against every of those things which are sinful; and therefore he shall apply himself the more vigorously to everything, that he may the more readily know how the flock fares, which he has to tend from God's hand; that the devil may not too greatly ravage therein, nor too much of his falsehood sow among them. Never will the people's course be well directed, nor well assured with regard to God, in that country where wrongful gain and most falsehood are loved; therefore should a friend of God suppress every unrighteousness, and exalt righteousness, and never consent that men, through falsehood and through wrongful gain, too greatly foredo themselves before the righteous God, who shuns every unrighteousness. It behoves all Christian men to love righteousness, and shun unrighteousness; and especially men in orders should ever exalt righteousness, and suppress unrighteousness; therefore should all bishops, with temporal judges, direct judgments so, that they never permit, if it be in their power, that

---

1. exculpation
2. 'burh' means 'castle'

any injustice spring up there. And on priests also it is incumbent, in their shrift-districts, that they diligently support every right, and never permit, if they can ameliorate it, that any Christian man too greatly injure another; nor the powerful the weak, nor the higher the lower, nor the shire man those under him, nor the *hlaford*[1] his men, not even his thralls. By the confessor's direction, and by his own measure, it is justly fitting that the thralls work for their *hlafords* over all the district in which he shrives. And it is right that there be not any measuring rod longer than another, but all regulated by the confessor's measure; and let every measure in his shrift-district and every weight be, by his direction, very rightly regulated: and if there be any dispute, let the bishop arbitrate. It is every *hlaford's* own advantage, to protect his thralls as he best may, because they and those that are free are equally dear to God, and he bought us all with equal value. We are all God's own thralls, and so he will judge us as we here judge those over whom we have judgment on earth: it therefore behoves us to protect those who are to obey us; then may we look for the greater protection at God's own judgment.

VIII. Likewise

A bishop's daily work.– That is rightly, his prayers first, and then his book-work, reading or writing, teaching or learning; and his church hours at the right time, always according to the things thereto befitting; and washing the feet of the poor; and his alms-dealing; and the direction of works, where it may be needful. Good handycrafts are also befitting him, that crafts may be cultivated in his family, at least that no one too idle may dwell there. And it also well befits him that at the *gemot*[2] he oft and frequently promulgate divine lore among the people with whom he then is.

---

1. lord
2. a mote or moot, meeting, public assembly

IX. Likewise

Wisdom and prudence are ever befitting bishops, and they have estimable ways who follow them; and that they also know some separate craft. Nothing useless ever befits bishops, neither extravagance, nor folly, nor too much drinking, nor childishness in speech, nor vain scurrility in any wise, neither at home, nor on a journey, nor in any place; but wisdom and prudence befit their order, and sobriety befits those who follow them.

It is incumbent on bishops in the synod, first of all to consider about unanimity and true concord among themselves, and how they may, before all things, exalt Christianity and most effectually suppress heathenism. And let every bishop have the book of canons at the synod. It is greatly needful to bishops, before God and before the world, that they all be strictly unanimous, and all desire one thing; and if any man do wrong to one, let all see it compensated. It is the duty of bishops to warn each other, if one hear anything of another, or know anything himself; and let each defend other behind his back; and no one conceal from another what it behoves him to know, but let each honour other by word and deed, and be, as it is their duty, *quasi cor unum et anima una.*

It is incumbent on bishops that venerable witan always travel with them, and dwell with them, at least of the priesthood; that they may consult with them, before God and before the world, and who may be their counsellors at every time, betide whatever betide them.

It is incumbent on bishops that there always be good instruction in their families and, be they where they may, let them be ever engaged on wisdom, and let alone every triviality unworthy of them.

It is incumbent on bishops not to be too prone to jesting, nor care too much for hounds and hawks, nor worldly pomp, nor vain pride.

It is incumbent on bishops not to be too eager for money at ordination, nor at consecration, nor at penance, nor in any wise to get wealth unjustly.

It is incumbent on bishops, if any one offend another, that he be patient until the arbitration of their associates, unless they can settle between themselves; and let them not refer to laymen, nor disgrace themselves.

It is incumbent on bishops, if aught greatly afflict anyone, for which he cannot obtain *bot*, that he make it known to his associates, and that they then be all diligent about the *bot*, and cease not before they have obtained it.

It is incumbent on bishops never to lay a curse upon any man, unless they are compelled by necessity; but if any one do it by compulsion, for enormous deeds, and the party will not yet yield to right, then let it be announced to all his associates, and then let them all lay on the same, and announce it to him; let him afterwards submit, and the more deeply make *bot*, if he reck of God's mercy and blessing.

It is incumbent on bishops, that they both rightly direct their own ways, and admonish to right men of every order.

It is incumbent on bishops patiently to endure what they themselves cannot amend, until it shall have been announced to the king; and let him then get amends for the offence against God, where the bishop cannot; if he will rightly execute God's will, and righteously exalt his own kingship.

XI. Of Eorls

Eorls and *heretogs*, and these secular judges, and likewise reeves, have need to love justice, before God and before the world, and nowhere, through unjust judgment, for money or for friendship, neglect their wisdom, so that they turn injustice to justice, or adjudge unjust judgment to the injury of the poor; but it is their duty, above all other things, to honour and defend the church, and gladden widows and step-children, and help the poor, and protect slaves, if they will rightly execute God's will; and thieves and public depredators they shall hate, and spoilers and robbers they shall condemn, unless they desist; and they shall ever rigidly shun injustice; for true it is what I say, believe it who will: woe to him who practises wrong too long; unless he desist, verily he shall traverse the dim and dark abyss of hell, of help deprived: but too few are there of those who that understand, as a man ought, but may God amend it; and let every friend do as is needful, let him diligently take heed, and guard himself, so that he anger God not too greatly, but propitiate his Lord with righteous deed.

XII. Of Reeves

It is right that reeves zealously provide, and always rightfully gain for their lords: but now it has been altogether too much the case, since Edgar ended, so as God willed it, that there are more robbers than righteous; and it is a grievous thing, that those are robbers who should be guardians of a Christian people. They rob the poor without any blame, and at another time devastate the flock that they ought to keep, and with evil pretexts defraud poor men, and set up unjust laws, in every wise to the injury of the poor; and oft and frequently strip widows. But whilom those men were chosen wisely in the nation, as guardians of the people, who would not, for worldly shame, nor durst, for fear of God, obtain anything by fraud, or make gain unjustly, but ever gained with justice: and since that it has been sought, by means of those above all, who knew how, most oppressively to cheat and deceive, and with falsehoods to injure poor men, and most speedily to get money from the innocent, since then God has been exceedingly much angered, oft and frequently; and woe to him, for his money, who has gained most of it by injustice, unless he desist, and the more deeply atone, before God and before the world.

XIII. Of Abbots

It is right that abbots, and especially abbesses, constantly dwell closely in their minsters, and ever zealously take care of their flocks, and always set them a good example, and rightly preach, and never about worldly cares, or vain pride either care too much or altogether too frequently; but oftenest busy themselves with ecclesiastical needs, as befits abbots and men of monkish order.

XIV. Of Monks

It is right that monks, by day and by night, with inward heart, ever think on God, and earnestly call upon him, and, with all humility, regularly live, and always separate themselves from worldly occupations, as they best may, and do as is their duty, ever care how they best may propitiate God, and all that perform which they promised, when they took order; to attend diligently to their books and prayers, to learn and to teach, as they best may; and every pomp, and vain pride, and separate property, and useless deed, and untimely speech wholly to despise, as is befitting monks. But it is truly an evil, as may be supposed, that some are too arrogant, and altogether too proud, and too widely erratic, and too useless, and altogether too idle in every good deed, and with regard to an evil deed, in secret profligacy, inwardly heartless, and outwardly indignant. And some are apostates, who ought, if they would, to be God's soldiers within their minsters; such are those who have cast off their [flocks], and who continue in worldly affairs, with sins. It [alas] goeth ill altogether too widely. So greatly doth it widely become worse among men, that those men in orders, who through fear of God, were whilom the most useful, and most laborious in divine ministry, and in book-craft, are now almost everywhere the most useless, and never labour strenuously on anything needful before God and before the world; but do all for lust and for ease, and love gluttony, and vain pleasure, stroll and wander, and all day trifle and talk and jest, and do nothing useful. That is a hateful life that they so lead; it is also the worse that the superiors do not amend it, nor some conduct themselves so well as they should; but it is our duty to amend it, as we most diligently may, and to be unanimous for the common need, before God and before the world.

XV. Of Mynchens

It is right that mynchens[1] behave monastically, even as we before said of monks, and not associate with secular men, nor too intimately have any separate acquaintance with them, but ever live according to their rule, and always separate themselves from worldly occupations, as they most diligently may.

XVI. Of Priests and Nuns

It is right that priests, and equally well nuns, live according to their rule, and preserve chastity, as they desire to dwell in a minster, or command respect before the world.

XVII. Of Widows

It is right that widows earnestly follow the example of Anna who was in the temple day and night, zealously serving: she fasted very often, and was devoted to prayers, and with groaning mind called to Christ, and distributed alms, oft and frequently, and ever propitiated God, as much as she was able, by word and deed, and has now for reward heavenly mirth. So should a good widow obey her Lord.

XVIII. Of God's Servants

Beloved men, hear I pray what I wish to say, through God's grace, for the need of us all, understand who can; and I pray you, beloved men, do as I enjoin; list very earnestly what I now say. To all Christian men it is much needful, that they follow God's law, and earnestly attend to divine instruction; and to men in orders

---

1.   a junior type of nun

especially it is of all most needful, because it is their duty earnestly both to preach and to exemplify God's righteousness to other men. Now will we earnestly enjoin God's servants, that they carefully bethink themselves, and through God's support, love chastity, and humbly serve God Almighty, and frequently pray for all Christian people, and that they diligently attend to books and prayers, and earnestly preach and exemplify God's righteousness, and that they enjoin frequently, as they may most diligently, that men in orders live according to their rule, and laymen lawfully direct their lives to their own benefit. And if it happen that misfortune befall the people, through an army, or famine, through plague, or mortality; through barrenness or storm; then let them earnestly consult how amends for this may be sought from Christ, with pure fasts, and with frequenting churches, and with humble prayers, and with alms-givings. And let them be always in harmony with themselves, and very unanimous, before God and before the world...

XIX. Of Priests

It is the duty of priests, in their shrift-districts, wisely and prudently to lead and teach the spiritual flocks, which they have to keep. They shall both well preach and give good example to other men; and they shall, at God's judgment, both give an account of their own deeds, and altogether of the people's whom, at God's hand, they have to keep; and if they shall have done aught, they may not flinch, neither for fear, nor for love of any man, from preaching righteousness and forbidding unrighteousness. Weak is the shepherd at the need of fold, who will not with his cry protect the flock that he has to keep, if there any public robber begin to rob. There is none so evil robber as is the devil himself; he is ever [busy] about that one thing, how he, among men's souls, may most devastate. Therefore must the shepherds be very watchful, and earnestly calling, who have to shield against the public spoiler. Those are bishops and mass-priests, who shall defend and protect the spiritual flock with wise instructions. Therefore he may not flinch, if he will secure himself, neither for love nor for fear, from saying to men what is most right. Nor may he flinch either before the lowly or the powerful, because he doeth naught, if he fear or be ashamed to speak righteousness. Ill will he fare, if through his lack of energy, the flock perish, which he has to keep, and himself along with it. Though any of our shepherds neglect but one sheep, we desire that he pay for it; but what, at God's awful judgment, shall then betide those shepherds, who cannot keep those spiritual flocks, that Christ bought with his own life, and which it is their duty to keep, if they can, but, through ignorance, can neither lead nor instruct, nor heal them rightly. With what do we expect they shall then pay for them? Woe to them then, that they ever undertook what they could not keep. Lo, how can one blind man lead another? How can an unlearned judge instruct another?...

XXIV. Of All Christian Men

It is right that all Christian men righteously hold their Christianity, and lead that life which is befitting them, according to God's law, and according to worldly conventions, and diligently order all their ways by those things which they direct, who are able wisely and prudently to direct them; and this then is first, of counsels foremost: that every man, above all other things, love one God, and stedfastly have one belief in him who first made us all, and with a dear price afterwards bought us. And also we have need earnestly to consider, how we may always most righteously hold God's own commandments, and perform all that which we promised, when we received baptism, or those who at our baptism were our sponsors. This then is first: that which we promise when we desire baptism... truly manifests that we will henceforth ever believe in one God, and constantly love him above all other things, and ever earnestly follow his instructions, and righteously hold his own commandments: and then will that baptism be as it were a pledge of all those words, and of all that promise, observe it who will. And true it is what I say, angels ever thenceforth watch every man, how he performs, after his baptism, that which he ere promised, when he desired baptism…

XXV. Of The Church

It is right that Christian men zealously hold Christianity with righteousness, and Christ's church everywhere zealously honour and protect. We all have one heavenly father, and one spiritual mother; she is named Ecclesia, that is God's church; and her we should ever love and honour. And it is right that every church be in God's *grith*[1] and in all Christian people's;… and every Christian man has great need that he show great reverence for that *grith*; because it is necessary for every Christian man zealously to love and honour God's church, and frequently and zealously to attend it, for his own benefit; and those in orders especially should there oftenest serve and minister, and earnestly intercede for all Christian people. Then have ministers of the altar constantly to consider that they, at all events, so order their lives as if justly fitting to the church. The church is rightly the priest's spouse… And no one should ever injure a church, or wrong it in any way; but now churches are, nevertheless, far and wide weakly 'grith'd', and ill-served, and cleanly bereft of their old rights, and within stript of all decencies; and ministers of the church are everywhere deprived of their rank and power; and woe to him who is the cause of this, though he may not think so; because everyone is certainly the foe of God himself, who is the foe of God's churches… Great is the necessity for every man, that he strenuously secure himself against these things; and let every friend of God constantly take care, that he do not too greatly misuse the bride of Christ. It is the duty of us all to love and honour one God, and zealously hold one Christianity, and with all our might renounce every heathenism.

---

1. peace, protection, particularly that granted by a king or other high official to those requiring it; also the privilege of security within a certain distance, ie within the verge of the king's court.

Index

117